FISHING CLOSE
TO THE BANK

FISHING CLOSE TO THE BANK

Robert (Bob) Cox

authorHOUSE®

AuthorHouse™ LLC
1663 Liberty Drive
Bloomington, IN 47403
www.authorhouse.com
Phone: 1-800-839-8640

Published by AuthorHouse   05/12/2014

ISBN: 978-1-4969-1104-9 (sc)
ISBN: 978-1-4969-1103-2 (e)

Lester Johnnie Cox 1924-2005

My dad, Lester Cox was the only person hired by the Idarado Mining Company in 1950. He held several positions at the mine, retiring in 1978 when the mine began closing down. Working as the hoistman on the T-Raise was one of Dad's first jobs. During that same time he also drove the company bus to the mine every day. He was a hard-working, self-educated man who somehow found time to take me hunting and fishing. We did not always get along, but we had an unwritten and unspoken agreement that all our problems were put aside during our hunting and fishing trips. It took me a long time to appreciate how important that was, but it is a lesson I will never forget and will continue to promote.

Photo from the Cox family collection.

Fishing Close to the Bank
Preface

What follows is not intended to be a comprehensive guide to fishing in Colorado. It is intended to entertain, and most of all, to pique the interest of the reader. The words are in many instances more metaphoric than literal.

Through my fishing and hunting stories I have tried over the years to impress upon my readers that we often do not have to look very far to achieve happiness. Sometimes, what we need and want most is right in front of us—close to the bank. We do not need to fill our baskets or our creels. We need only enough to replenish our bodies and keep our souls active.

While I am not an advocate of always practicing "catch and release," sometimes letting our quarry go is the best way to capture its essence. I respect life, but I am a realist in the sense that I am part of the animal kingdom. I have been blessed with being put at the top of the food chain, but I never take that for granted. Every time I eat a fish or sit down to an elk steak, I thank God for the sustenance that it provides me and I am constantly thankful that I have been able to take advantage of the world around me. All of the photos are mine, unless otherwise noted in the captions.

I have laid aside business, and gone a-fishing

(Izaac Walton)

A ceramic mug with the likeness of Izaak Walton is as close to the 17ᵗʰ century author as I will ever get. His book, *The Compleat Angler,* was published in 1653. My copy is only about 100 years old, but I still enjoy connecting with Walton and his fishing stories.

While at a seminar early in 2004, I met Case Hicks. Hicks was traveling around the country imitating Theodore Roosevelt and promoting conservation. I started thinking about how much fun he was having and how much fun I could have if I could do something similar to what he was doing.

Being Roosevelt would be a kick. I have a lot of the same interests Roosevelt had, but it would be tacky for me to go off doing a re-enactment of the same person. I wanted to come up with someone else; someone with whom I could connect on a basic level. I wanted to find someone who loved to fish and/or hunt and was famous enough to spark some interest.

Later in the year, while keeping up to date on the Democratic Convention being held in Boston, I learned that impersonators of historical figures were in big demand. One man who portrays Ben Franklin was asked to oversee a poorly represented re-enactment of the Boston Tea Party. Another was summoned to use his personification of Paul Revere to promote gun control. Ben took the job, Paul turned the offer down. At any rate, that renewed my desire to emulate someone.

I was about 12 years old when I first read *The Compleat Angler*, written by Izaak Walton. I remember enjoying it, but mostly I remember that the local librarian would not allow me to check out any other books written by Walton unless my parents said it was okay. She said that some of what he wrote was not appropriate for a person of my impressionable age. That did it. I read everything he had written, and I have re-read them over the years.

Walton loved to fish and his essay-style in *The Compleat Angler* offered advice on just about any type of fishing one could think of. Some of his fly-fishing techniques are as good today as they were in 1653 when the book was first published. Maybe I could become Izaak Walton. The problem is that Walton lived a life style that I don't think I could pretend to be comfortable with. I think that is why Mrs. Kuchs (the librarian) thought I should not read his work. Besides, I really don't look much like Walton and, as far as I know, he never fished in the USA, let alone the Gunnison River. I do, however, prescribe to his statement in the first chapter:

"Doubt not but angling will prove to be so pleasant that it will prove to be, like virtue, a reward to itself."

My next choice of a person whom I could imitate was Ernest Hemingway. Hemingway's father taught him very early to enjoy fishing and hunting. He spent a considerable time pursuing both hobbies in the woods and forests near Lake Michigan. He was a big fan of Theodore Roosevelt, and went to Africa in 1933 to hunt big game after reading Roosevelt's accounts of such adventures.

That trip provided fodder him to write another of my favorite stories, *The Short Happy Life of Francis Macomber.*

No, Hemingway will not work either. He did something that really disgusts me. He committed suicide in 1961. That doesn't make his whole life wrong, and I still enjoy re-reading some of his novels, but I just don't think I could be Hemingway.

What I can do is be myself, and that means enjoying the area in which I live. I can literally plan and execute a fishing trip on the spur of the moment. I don't need an African safari. I can hunt elk within a few miles of home. I don't need permission from the King to fish in royal waters. I can drive into the national forest, walk up the bank of a clear stream and catch a few brook trout before breakfast. Who knows, maybe I am already acting like Izaak Walton and Ernest Hemingway.

I always hated the parts in creative writing and literature classes when the teacher or professor would require that the motives of the author of some work be scrutinized and his or her reasons for writing are subject to second-guessing. I always wanted to think that Mark Twain wrote *Huckleberry Finn* because it was a great story and because he loved to tell stories. I rejected the thought that Twain was grasping for freedom from the turmoil of life and was using the Mississippi River as an example of that freedom. Now I am not so sure. When I began to reflect on my reasons for writing what I write, I also began to wonder if other people would see through those reasons and see me for what I really am. First, and foremost, I am a storyteller, but I have to admit that most of my stories have basis and reason that go beyond the story itself. What follows is no different.

How often do we plan our lives around a wish that we were actually someone else, living in another place and possessing what we do not have and likely will never achieve? I still think it would be a kick in the pants to run around portraying a famous man, but we have to be careful that we do not give up what we have in the vain and unproductive pursuit of that which we are not destined to achieve.

Does that mean we should not pursue dreams? Absolutely not. Dreams are what life is made of. Pursuit of happiness is one of those "certain inalienable rights" upon which our forefathers founded an entire nation. But wishing away our lives can be detrimental to those dreams.

If the truth is known, I would almost rather that the reader of this effort stop right here and read *The Compleat Angler* before going on. I said "almost" because I certainly do not want to dissuade anyone from partaking of the words that follow. I do, however want to stress the fact that, had it not been for my reading of the aforementioned work, I likely would not be doing what I am today.

The first part of *The Compleat Angler* is primarily dedicated to the conversations of three companions who, owing to circumstance, happened to travel together for several days. Each of the three had a passion for a particular sport, and each agreed to pass his knowledge of that sport to his companions. Each of the travelers agreed to not intentionally find fault with the other's recreation. One was an angler, one a hunter and the other a falconer.

Just as each of these three travelers imparted his respective knowledge to his companions, we would be well advised to spend some time talking about, and even participating in things of which we have little or no interest. The results can be satisfying.

I am not a golfer, nor do I have any interest in becoming one. I did try to play the game a time or two many years ago. I just could not become interested in it. I thought then, and think now, that doing that much walking without a fishing rod or a rifle made little sense. I have friends who are dedicated golfers. Some of them also hunt and fish; some have no desire to do either. Over the last few years I enjoyed listening to them talk about golf and have even come to a point where I understand some of the terms. I came to a conclusion: most golfers are pretty honest people. As in hunting or fishing, golf has no referees. Each participant is responsible for keeping his own score and accurately spotting the location of his last shot. Integrity and ethics go a long way in the world of golfers, hunters and fishermen, yet I will not deny the tendency of all of them to enhance the stories of their last outing, especially if there is no one present to dispute the claims. I really don't have a problem with a little fish story about the one that got away or a golfer claiming that a seagull swooped down and stole a ball that was put on the green on the second shot. My point is that the game was played fair in the first place. More often than not, that is the case.

My point to all this is simple: We are often tempted with the prospect of trying to be someone we are not. So many people go through life trying to convince everyone that they are another Theodore Roosevelt or Winston Churchill or Ernest Hemingway. They forget to be themselves. They spend all their waking moments behind a self-made mask that prevents others from seeing them for what they really are. Often, when their masquerade is exposed, they are mistrusted and pushed to the outside of their circle of friends without ever knowing the reason why.

By the same token, we are easily convinced, usually by our own thoughts and actions, that our way is the right way, to the exclusion of every other methodology. We fail to recognize that learning to appreciate what others enjoy, and sharing ideas with others who have dissimilar beliefs, can do nothing less than expand our own horizons. Time is never wasted if something new is learned, regardless of how mundane it may seem at the time.

CHAPTER TWO

Cow Creek

Long impressive casting has no place on some of the small creeks that I grew up fishing. Short fly rods and short roll casts are the order of the day, and when that fails, an ultra-light spinning rod and a small spinner might well be the better choice. Though Cow Creek runs from being a raging torrent in the spring to barely a trickle late in the summer, like many smaller streams it will give up some impressive fish if you just do not forget to fish close to the bank, or in this case the cliff.

Cow Creek begins its life near the southernmost boundary of what is now known as the Uncompahgre Wilderness Area, formerly the Big Blue Wilderness. I always found it interesting that the headwaters of Cow Creek begin almost on top of the 38th Parallel.

While there is some interest in fishing in the Big Blue, most of the focus is on Big Blue Creek in an entire different drainage than that of Cow Creek. Terrain and private property makes Cow Creek a challenge, but one I love to engage in once in a while.

In its early stages, Cow Creek collects water from several smaller creeks high in the south of Wildhorse Peak, which reaches up and touches the sky at just over 13,000 feet. Among the little feeders are Wildhorse Creek, Wetterhorn Creek and Difficulty Creek. There is a small finger of non-wilderness national forest land that reaches south into the wilderness from just south of Courthouse Creek to where Oben Creek joins Cow Creek. This is one of the few opportunities to access Cow Creek from a road, which is just over 3 miles long, but the fishing is not always good.

As Cow Creek gathers the run-off of all those little creeks, it falls at a significant rate and can become a raging torrent of water that belies its five or so miles of existence before getting to the forest boundary. The road north of the boundary is subject to massive washouts and is often impassable, although using an ATV expands the possibilities somewhat.

For all intents and purposes Cow Creek spends most of its remaining course crossing private land, including the famous Sleeping Indian Ranch. The only exception is a short piece that flows through the Beckett Tract of the Billy Creek Wildlife Area and another short flow through the Ridgway State Park below the Pa Co Chu Puk camping area.

As a young man, I had a lot more access to the creek than I do now, but I still love fishing it. The creek ranges, depending on the time of the year and weather, from a raging, boulder-rolling flood, to barely enough water to see any flow at all. All that said, I have taken some nice 12-inch natives out of the upper parts of the creek and more than one 16-inch brown trout from the lower reaches.

There are a few nice holes but fishing Cow Creek is usually not a daylong excursion, which is exactly why I like it. I can leave home, fish for an hour and be back before anyone knows I am gone.

One of the most gratifying things about spending time hunting and fishing is the observation of wildlife and the lessons that can be applied to everyday living. I know some people think there is a conflict in my thinking. I enjoy a good venison steak, but I also enjoy watching deer in their natural environment and I am sincere in my desire to protect wild animals. I simply understand that man is part of the animal kingdom and that hunting and fishing is actually a good thing for our wildlife. Life's lessons are well taught in Mother Nature's classroom. Cow Creek afforded me one of those once-in-a-lifetime experiences and a lesson in life.

Several years ago, while fishing Cow Creek, I took a detour around some rather nasty willows. As I worked my way back to the creek I heard a sound that I could not immediately identify. It almost sounded like a person who was wheezing. I moved slowly into a willow thicket to investigate. What I found was one of the most amazing things I had ever encountered. A young doe deer was in the last minutes of giving birth. I literally stood and watched as she did her part to ensure the mule deer population. After quite literally witnessing the miracle of life, I backed off and left the mother and her newborn. For several days I thought about going back to that spot just to see if I could see the young one again. I did not go, mostly because I did not think it was a good idea to disturb the newborn or its mother.

My children were among the last generation when fathers did not go into the delivery room. We were relegated to pacing back and forth in an adjoining room, which was aptly named "the waiting room." Wait we did; and smoked one cigarette after another. I am not exaggerating. Smoking was allowed in hospitals back then. That was way back in the late 60s and early 70s. Today the cigarettes have been kicked out and the father, sister, mother of the mother and anyone else who may have received an invitation are herded into the delivery room and encouraged to bring video cameras and notebooks. The birth of a child seems to have become somewhat of a spectator sport.

Before I give the wrong impression, let me explain something. I think it is great that a father is in the delivery room with his wife and gets to witness this special event and I think it does create a special bond, which is shared between mother, father and baby. I also think a young woman's mother should be available if at all possible to give advice and comfort to her daughter, especially the first time around. Beyond that, I am not sure. And, as for the video, that seems to me to be somewhat bizarre.

Maybe those who have been part of this human process would not have been as impressed as I was with what I had observed that day in those willows. I had witnessed cows giving birth, and had even assisted once when a calf needed to be pulled, but somehow this was different. It was nature at its purest and in my mind it made me special.

I cannot help but become somewhat perturbed at various animal rights groups who constantly tie their individual agendas to purported demise of some creature. Their real causes often have nothing to do with the animal they are supposedly trying to protect and they often carry their protests to ridiculous lengths. As a sportsman that hunts and fishes, I want to stand up and yell to these people that people like me are the reason that people like them can do what they do. Without our true conservation of the wildlife, things would be drastically different.

CHAPTER THREE

I've got a secret—Crystal Lake

Crystal Lake, located at the north end of Ironton Park on Highway 550's famous Million Dollar Highway, was for many years a private lake that tempted local residents. It is now public and provides both beauty and fishing opportunity.

The Million Dollar Highway south of the town of Ouray is probably one of the most well known stretches of Colorado mountain highway. The 24 miles from Ouray to Silverton traverses through narrow canyons with sheer drops to the river. The traveler of Highway 550 leaves Ouray at just under 7,800 feet above sea level and travels 12 miles to the top of Red Mountain Pass at 11,018 feet, and then descends down the other side another 12 miles to Silverton, which rests at a lofty 9,318 feet.

About five miles from Ouray the road becomes almost level, crossing a huge high park where Red Mountain Creek flows north. Its rusty red color epitomizes the evidence of high concentrates of iron in the surrounding mountains. Three of those mountains, Red Mountain One, Two and Three, stick up into an often-pure blue sky, giving the impression that they have been painted red. The iron literally flows down their slopes. At the north end of the park is a beautiful lake that shows none of the red iron color because it is not fed by Red Mountain Creek, but rather by the other small tributaries on the west side of the valley.

It is a pure blue-green that on a calm day will reflect the mountains above across its surface with an awe-inspiring beauty. At one time there was talk of a dam that would have filled much of the park with a lake. I will talk a little more about that in another chapter.

A short distance south of the lake a few old buildings mark what is left of the town of Ironton, which was once populated with over 1,000 people involved in the local mining industry. On December 18, 1961, E.O. Milton Larson appeared on the television show *I've Got a Secret*. The show's normal host was Gary Moore, but on that day Henry Morgan was filling in, leading a panel to guess what Larson's "secret" was. Larson, a humorous eccentric, whom I remember well, finally shared his secret when he told the audience that he was the sole resident of the town of Ironton, Colorado. He was also the mayor and the postmaster. I think he died in about 1965 and the town was no longer incorporated. I helped Johnny Johnson clean out some of the artifacts from Ironton to be placed in the Western Hotel Museum in Ouray.

All that is interesting and now we all know one of the secrets of Ironton, but I just happen to know another one.

That lake I mentioned is officially known as Crystal Lake, but when I was growing up at about the time Larson was the mayor in Ironton, Crystal Lake and the surrounding property was owned by a religious group commonly known as the "I Ams." More accurately, the property was owned by the parent organization, the Saint Germain Foundation. Trespassing was strictly forbidden, but the knowledge that the lake was home to some legendary large trout made staying away rather difficult for some people.

One such person was a man I will only refer to as Charlie. Most of my pals and I knew that Charlie was prone to night excursion to the "I Am Lake." Well, on one of his nocturnal outings, Charlie managed to land a huge trout. Charlie could not resist bragging a little about the fish, but telling where he caught it would be admitting to criminal activity, so he told people he caught it in the Uncompahgre River north of town. Everyone, including the local newspaper, picked up on the story. I will have to give it to Charlie, he kept to his guns and to his secret, but we all knew better.

The Saint Germain Foundation ultimately sold the property to some Ouray investors. They, likewise did not allow any fishing and in fact drained the lake down and made it abundantly clear that there were no fish in it.

Several years ago the property became part of the Uncompahgre National Forest. The lake was revitalized and has since been drained and restocked again. It is a great place to pull off the side of the road and fish for a couple of hours. I especially enjoy putting out my inflatable one-man pontoon boat and lurking around the lake in pursuit of one of the brook or cutthroats that now inhabit the water. Those typical high mountain lake flies work the best. Try a wooly worm or coachman pattern, and maybe, just maybe you will become part of the Ironton Park legend.

CHAPTER FOUR

Eleven Mile—Blizzards, Bikinis and Basketball

Eleven Mile Reservoir in South Park is an important part of the Denver Water System. The water backed up behind the 147-foot dam is also one of the most popular recreation areas in Colorado. Each year the operator of the Eleven Mile Marina hosts a series of ice fishing tournaments, one of which has taken on the moniker of March Madness. The ice fishing enthusiasts score points, not just based on the fish they catch, but also on the number of free-throws they can sink through the basketball goals set up on the ice.

I do not know Larry Faulk real well, but I know him well enough to know that he is one of those people who can turn lemons into lemonade. Faulk is the concessionaire that runs the marina at Eleven Mile Reservoir.

I have a special sort of connection with Eleven Mile. I was born in Cripple Creek and my family on my mother's side are among the founders of both Florissant and Fairplay, smack in the middle of Colorado's South Park where the wind never stops blowing and the winters are as harsh as anyplace in Colorado, or for that matter a lot of other places.

Zebulon Pike tried to climb Pike's Peak during his 1806 exploration, but it was not until the mid 1850s that the area around South Park became the focus of some very brave people. The first full-gauge railroad in the Colorado Rocky Mountains, the Midland, was built in 1887. Everyone knows that gold and silver are what made Colorado, but the fact is that water has been every bit as important as those precious minerals. No sooner had the settlers began to move into the state than they began to realize that, while they were flowing in, the water was flowing out. Some took advantage of the downhill makeup of Colorado and began making some questionable arrangements with the states into which the water was flowing. For others, keeping the water stored in Colorado became paramount.

The 147 feet high dam that backs water up into Eleven Mile Reservoir was built in 1932. The water is an important part of the Denver Water Department. While the primary purpose of storing the water is to provide Denver with drinking water, along with some irrigation, the lake has become a major recreation area and is now managed as such by the Colorado Parks and Wildlife.

Ice fishing has not always been legal in Colorado. The state used to have a fishing season that precluded any winter fishing at all. Even after the sport became legal, it took quite some time before it really became popular. For years, the activity around Eleven Mile dwindled to nothing as the snows began to fall and the lake froze over. There were a brave few who ventured out onto the ice, but they were often looked at as though they should be housed in a secure facility for their own protection.

When Faulk took over the marina it was basically a summer only enterprise. He changed that in a big way. In cooperation with the CPW, Faulk began holding three ice-fishing tournaments each winter. In order to be the big winner, one must participate in all three tournaments, but good prizes are awarded in each separate tournament also. I have never entered the January and February tournaments, but I am here to tell you that the March tournament, which has taken on the moniker "March Madness," is indeed madness and often a whole lot of fun.

Faulk and his staff set up two basketball goals on the ice. During each weigh-in session teams shoot free throws in order to acquire more points and a better chance for prize money. That activity alone often kept me from getting close to the prize money. I shoot guns and photographs, not basketballs.

As can happen the weather was great during the 2008 March Madness. I did not have a teammate, but they have that covered also. Those who show up without teammates simply pair up for the day. It is a great way to meet new people—most of the time. So, here we are drilling holes through more than 30 inches of ice and trying to entice that big rainbow that will tip the scales in our favor. Suddenly we are interrupted with a sweet "good morning." Much to my surprise there stood before me a cute little thing dressed in a bikini and snow boots. Julie Noy, a 23-year-old pre-med student, was helping Faulk out with public relations and marketing and she was doing a bang-up job.

Like I said, I don't shoot basketballs, but I know someone who does. Ray Markey and I have been friends since we were infants. We went to school from kindergarten together and graduated among a class of 20 from Ouray High School. That year of our graduation, Ray's photo appeared in our school yearbook with the caption "Most Athletic." Ray was a basketball player and he and I had ventured off on more than one fishing trip. It didn't take long to convince Ray that he should go with me to the 2009 tournament. The photos of Julie Noy helped considerably.

While the 2008 weather was conducive to the scant costume of one young lady, the 2009 weather certainly was not. At 7 a.m. the morning of the tournament we found ourselves drilling holes in the ice while trying to keep our backs to a 20 mph wind that was blowing across bare ice and gusting to the point that standing up was a challenge at times. Shortly after the tournament started one team landed the first fish of the day and netted a $59 prize. That helped keep us watching our holes. At 8 a.m. the first weigh-in horn sounded and thus the first round of basketball action. It was our time to shine. Ray did the shooting for our team. We decided earlier that I was the fishing expert and he was the basketball expert. He missed both shots. He made some excuse about the wind and we returned to our ice holes, having not even placed in the first round.

The trout available from Eleven Mile are as colorful as they are good tasting. Their diets are such that the meat is dark pink much like their salmon cousins.

Before the tournament was half over and with us having very little to show for our efforts, Ray was nearly frozen to his chair. He looked up at me, grinning through the ice crystals around his nose and said, "Okay Cox, tell me one more time about this lady in the bikini." I could tell the day was over. We packed up and headed into Hartsel, where we enjoyed some sausage and eggs and plenty of hot coffee before tackling the four hour trip back home.

Fishing through the ice at Eleven Mile is great sport. The typical ice jigs, mealworms and wax worms are always good choices. There are some sizable northern pike in the lake, much to the chagrin of many of us. If catching one of the pike is your purpose, I suggest getting some sucker meat and suspend it at the end of a wire leader. Fish finders and underwater cameras are great tools at Eleven Mile. There is a lot of lake to cover and finding the fish is important. Be ready for some nice two and three pound rainbows that have orange meat that rivals their salmon cousins. They are great eating, not something I will say about all rainbows. I always keep one or two of the Eleven Mile trout, which I grill on a cedar board.

CHAPTER FIVE

Remembering the Highland Marys

The small peninsula at the left of the photo is one of my favorite spots when fishing Highland Mary Lake #1. On one occasion my friends and I used this spot for a very unique form of "trolling." My thanks to Jan Studebaker for the photo. It is much better than the ones in my collection.

I always considered growing up in the little town of Ouray, Colorado to be a privilege. In fact, I often thought that everyone else was just unlucky to have grown up elsewhere. I know now that most people who had a long-time relationship with their childhood town feels pretty much the same way I do, but to me Ouray will always be special.

I hate to paint everyone with a broad brush, but I see little evidence today that the young people, even in very small towns, have the freedoms that my friends and I had during our formative years.

My parents moved to Ouray from Cripple Creek in late 1949 when I was a mere six months old. My dad was the only person hired by the Idarado Mining Company in 1950. He worked there until the mine began closing down in 1978. During my childhood years, Ouray enjoyed a fairly stable economic environment. Fourteen of the twenty kids in my high school graduation class started kindergarten together. That kind of stability is not nearly as common today as it was then.

My dad, Lester Cox, enjoyed going hunting and fishing, largely I believe because of his early association with my mother's family. The Bielz family was renowned for its outdoor activity. They were constantly camping, hunting and fishing. Some of that heritage found its way into my bloodstream and the area around Ouray presented a great opportunity to take advantage of, and enjoy, the outdoors.

Among Dad's favorite fishing spots were a group of lakes above Silverton. For many of his years at the mine Dad worked a schedule of two weeks on day shift, and then switched to two weeks of night shift. On one or two of the long-change weekends of each summer, when he would leave the mine on Friday evening and not have to be back to work until Monday night, a couple of his friends and he would go directly from work to fishing. They would drive from the Idarado on top of Red Mountain Pass to Silverton and hike into the Highland Mary Lakes, where they would, as related to me by Dad, spend a rather cool night, fish for a few hours the next morning and return home, often by noon.

Quite often those trips yielded a basket full of beautifully colored native cutthroat trout. Several times I watched Dad at the kitchen sink getting some of the fish ready for mom to cook. They put the extra ones into pans of water so they could be frozen for later feasts.

I remember only one trip into the Highland Mary Lakes with Dad, but I later made almost yearly trips with friends. The last time I hiked in was with my eldest son, more years ago than I like to admit.

More often than not, we chose to take fly rods on these trips. Most of us also adapted hunting coats into fishing equipment storage and packing devices. The many pockets provided convenient places to put extra tackle and the large game pouch on the back made a perfect creel. The canvas duck material provided a certain amount of protection from the frequent storms. My aluminum fly rod case sometimes doubled as a walking stick. While we enjoyed using flies, we were also practical thinkers and we always had a tobacco can loaded up with a dozen or so nice juicy worms. In one of the coat pockets, I carried a bait-casting reel. By removing the tip from the fly rod and attaching the bait-casting reel, I could fashion a very usable bait fishing rig that, notwithstanding the inevitable backlashes, served me rather well over the years.

One trip sticks in my memory more than others, probably because I tell the story at every opportunity. Two friends and I left Ouray long before daylight, in fact it was still dark when we arrived at the trailhead to the Highland Mary Lakes. We loaded our coats up with the necessary sandwiches, tackle and toilet paper and made an uneventful trip up the mountain.

Fishing these high mountain lakes is always a hit-and-miss situation. For our purposes, the best fishing days were those when there were a few clouds temporarily blocking the sun and maybe even a short afternoon rain shower. On that particular day there was not a cloud in the sky. There was no breeze and rising trout did little to disturb the tranquil surface of the lake. In short, it was a great day to fish, but not a very good day to catch. We even tried putting a worm on a hook and resting it on the bottom of the lake, but that yielded exactly zero fish. Then, while searching through my various pieces of tackle in my coat, I found a small set of copper pop gear. We rigged the pop gear up with a worm on the end, much like we would have done if we were trolling it behind a boat, and tried casting it out into the lake, using the aforementioned method of taking the tip off the fly rod. The setup was not very conducive to casting and made a hell of mess of the line on that old casting reel.

Highland Mary Lake Number One is shaped somewhat like a very misshapen heart and the familiar "dent" in this case is a small protrusion of land into the waters of the lake. It was one of my favorite spots for fly-fishing because it allowed for my somewhat clumsy back casts. Following some very innovative thinking, we decided to rig up the pop gear with a worm, and then have one person stand out on the tip of that protrusion while another took the end of the line and walked around to the opposite shore, dropping the spinners into the water and allowing the person with the rod to retrieve them across a substantial amount of deep and productive water. It worked better than our wildest dreams. We began taking turns with who did the reeling and who walked around to the other bank. One after another, those 16-inch natives grabbed the worm and became part of our daily bag limit. I don't remember exactly how many fish we caught, but our game pouches were overflowing and we had a blast telling people that we caught a mess of fish while "trolling" the Highland Mary.

Highland Mary Number One sits at about 12,000 feet elevation. To get there, turn up the highway to Howardsville from Silverton to Forest Service Road 589 to Cunningham Gulch. At the end of the road, head up the trail. We always claimed the hike to be four miles, but I don't think it is quite that far. The area is smack dab in the middle of the Weminuche Wilderness area and today is used by a significant number of stick-walkers, but it surprises me how many of them are just out for the hike and do not really take the time to stop and fish for an hour or two. Don't forget the worms.

CHAPTER SIX

Ridgway Reservoir—A Town Saved and Some Quality Time With Dad

During the construction phase of Ridgway Dam, my family and I had an opportunity to tour the construction site. I charted and photographed much of the lakebed, hoping to someday turn my information into valuable fishing knowledge. For a large part, it worked. This is the lakebed just prior to the lake filling with water.

I really cannot remember when I first heard about a plan to put a dam on the Uncompahgre River below Ridgway. I do remember a lot of talk about it for many years and I personally heard Wayne Aspinal give a speech or two that included the plan.

Aspinal, while a Democrat at the time, was a very conservative Democrat and was well liked by most Ouray County people, largely because of his strong commitment to water storage. He also believed that the local and state governments needed to have more control of the federal lands. The environmentalists of the 1950s and 1960s probably did not like him much.

In the late 1940s, after World War II, the Bureau of Reclamation had some serious talks about damming up the waters of the upper Uncompahgre. The project was called the Ouray Project, but was never published and information is largely based on as much rumor as fact. As I understand it, a dam catching the waters of the headwaters of the Uncompahgre, Red Mountain Creek and several other small creeks at the north end of Ironton Park would have basically turned the park into one huge lake. The project did not go far because it simply did not serve the agricultural community enough and feasibility was a major problem. What the Ouray Project did do is keep the conversations about water storage going. The result was the Dallas Project, authorized by the Colorado River Storage Project Act of 1956.

As Aspinal and his supporters first envisioned the Dallas Project, it would have inundated the town of Ridgway with the high water line stretching well south of town. Many an argument about the pros and cons of the project took place over coffee and donuts at the Little Chef Café in Ridgway. I remember one such conversation involving Aspinal himself while I sat with my dad and a few of his friends.

Ultimately, the Dallas Project was approved in 1968, but the controversy and arguments raged on. The project finally started in 1978 and was completed in 1987. I spent the years from 1969 to 1980 on the Eastern Plains of Colorado near Burlington. When we moved to Montrose in 1980, Ridgway Reservoir became one of my focal points. I watched anxiously as the project progressed. I sat on the side of the hill at an old gravel pit and anticipated the lake and the day that all the dirt and rock would be covered with water. The lake filled in 1990 and I had another place to go fishing.

I don't think I have ever researched a fishing spot like I did Ridgway. Almost every time I visited the area during the construction, I marked up some maps and charted those special areas that I knew would some day hold fish.

At the time, I had a 12-foot aluminum boat with a 7.5 h.p. motor. It was more than adequate for the type of fishing I was doing, but Ridgway Reservoir seemed to shout out to me that I needed something bigger. Besides, I wanted to be able to take a couple of friends and especially my dad and be comfortable while fishing. My kids were at an age when I thought they might also enjoy a bigger boat.

Art Dougherty, the longtime sheriff of Ouray County had a boat stored in an old garage in Colona owned by Billy Hotchkiss. It didn't take me long after the lake filled to begin negotiating with Art for his boat. He was not using it and I certainly had the perception of needing it. As I saw it, that 83,000 acre-feet of water needed some attention from me. Ultimately, Art and I reached an agreement and I became the proud owner of a 16 foot long, 1970 Larson Boat with an 85 h.p. Johnson outboard.

After finally getting the motor to run decently, and replacing all the wheel bearings and the tires on the trailer, I installed a state-of-the art sonar fish finder. It had all the bells and whistles of the time and I was convinced it was the secret to finding those special places at Ridgway Reservoir. I was not disappointed.

Dad and I spent many days trolling along just the right places, near just the right structure. We noted landmarks to coincide with the notes and pictures I took while the dam was being built. We caught fish and had a blast doing it. Many a time we would arrange to meet after we both got off work in an evening and fish for two or three hours.

A favorite activity for both Dad and I was to gather up an old friend, Joe Smart and go night fishing at Ridgway. I mounted some old sealed beam spotlight bulbs in chunks of Styrofoam that we floated beside the boat. We baited up with the biggest night crawlers we could find and used big black doll fly jigs straight down under the boat. Today's LED lights will probably work even better than the ones we used then. Keep in mind that this is a catch and keep style of fishing, but we knew that and knew we were blessed with an opportunity to have a few good meals of trout after one of these late nights. The stories told by Dad and Joe were worth the trips even had we not caught a single fish.

After Dad's health began to decline and the kids moved out, I used the boat less and less. It was wet from rain on top more often than from lake water on the bottom. I decided to sell it. In the long run, I practically gave the thing away. Selling old boats is not an easy thing to do. I don't remember whom I sold it to, but years later I saw that old boat parked in a farmyard along a road I still travel frequently. It just sits there with weeds growing up around it. They (whoever they are) moved it farther away from the road a few years ago, but there is no evidence it has been used for at least the last 12 years or so. I cannot help thinking of my dad and the time we spent together in that boat. It is so sad to see it parked there with no father, no friends and no kids. It is made of heavy fiberglass so it cannot even rust away into history.

The casual fisherman never sees much of the structure of any lake. Note that the high water line is well above the cliffs, but knowing exactly where those cliffs are, makes the pursuit of the brown trout that hide there just that much easier.

Ridgway is still one of my favorite destinations. The dam's final location saved the town of Ridgway, but many of the property owners had given up and it took more than a few years for the town to become the vibrant little fork in the road that it is today.

I became soft over the years and enjoy taking a travel trailer once in awhile and spending a few days at Ridgway Reservoir, but I no longer go out on the lake too far. I am limited to where I can paddle around on my one-man pontoon boat. I still know those secret places and I still know that a black doll fly on the right autumn day, in just the right place, will result in a 16-20 inch brown trout and that is just enough fish for Diane and I to have a truly special gourmet meal. It may be 83,000 acre feet of water, but I have it figured out and every day I spend there results in one more memory that can be stored in the archives of a special life.

CHAPTER SEVEN

Uncompahgre River—Weighing the Benefits and Maybe a Few Fish

The Uncompahgre River is much different today than it was in the years before Ridgway Dam was constructed. This stretch just below the dam has become a very popular year-around fishery where hooking up with three to five pound trout is a common experience.

I am no different than most people. I sometimes would like to have things both ways. I know that can never happen, but I always seem to hold out for the possibility.

Back in 1909 the Uncompahgre Valley witnessed a drastic change. The change came in the form of water. A gargantuan project involved drilling a tunnel from the Gunnison River at the bottom of the Black Canyon and diverting a substantial amount of water from the Gunnison River into the Uncompahgre Valley. The overall project fed numerous canals and irrigation ditches and literally brought the valley to life.

While lots of people see where the water is diverted through the tunnel at the East Portal, relatively few have actually seen where it comes out on the west side. I have had the pleasure of seeing both, and have done some enjoyable research on the project itself. I even have an old glass slide depicting President Howard Taft performing the ceremonial opening of the tunnel.

About a half of a mile below the West Portal, the water from the tunnel enters into the main part of the South Canal. The force of the water going down the various shoots and through some smaller tunnels is an awesome sight. Between where the water starts running in the canal and where it dumps into the Uncompahgre River several miles south, there have been unique opportunities for fishermen.

Although providing a fishery was no part of the original plan, the South Canal became a popular place for locals to go. The fish that found their way into the tunnel, and thereafter the canal, also made it into the Uncompahgre River, making the river south of Montrose a lot better, although most of it is on private property and not easy to get access to. I could literally leave my house and be fishing in the canal within minutes, and I often did just that.

Several years ago the Delta Montrose Electric Association proposed placing one or more hydroelectric generators into the canal system. The force in which the water enters the canal certainly lends itself to the production of hydropower. I found myself torn between two factions on this. I am a big proponent of the small hydroelectric projects. They certainly make more sense than burning algae in my Dodge pickup. There was a certain group of persons who wanted to see the hydroplant washed away in favor of keeping the fishing opportunity. There were also those who wanted to see the hydropower developed without any consideration of the loss of fishing opportunity in the South Canal and the Uncompahgre River.

The necessary installation of the penstock and rerouting of the water below the West Portal of the Gunnison Tunnel that provided for the first power plant became a reality in 2013. Because the fish cannot survive a trip through the turbines, they are prevented from entering the tunnel at the East Portal. There are no more fish in the South Canal, but mitigation efforts are being implemented and us hooky players are not completely left out of the system.

Through some great efforts on the part of local residents and the Colorado Parks and Wildlife, fishing opportunities are getting better on the Uncompahgre River. In fact, there are great places to fish that are actually within the city limits of Montrose. The mitigation stocking started in late 2013 from the point at which the South Canal dumps into the Uncompahgre to the Highway 90 Bridge on the western edge of Montrose. I am always cautious about giving specific instructions as to access. Be sure to check if there is any doubt about public access. Trespassing is taken seriously in Colorado, and well it should be. There is some good access near the Chipeta Ute Indian Museum and through Baldridge Park. I find that going during a weekday usually results in very little interaction with other anglers.

Here again, those dyed in the wool really serious fly fishermen cringe at me once in awhile, but I don't always rely only on my fly rod. When I do, I find that all the summer fly patterns work pretty well, but come winter, plan on using some really small offerings. I often tie three or four on separate tippets and change the whole tippet rather than trying to handle a size 18 or 22 fly when the cold air takes what little feeling I still have out of my fingertips. The Copper Johns seem to work well and most any of the midges, including the Zebra and the Blue Winged Olive patterns.

A spinning rod is not a bad thing on this newly revived stretch of river. Cast the small silver Mepps or Rooster tails upstream into the deeper pools and you may be surprised what comes back out. You want a nice brown for supper, take a few minutes to thread a piece of a night crawler on a hook and drift it through one of those deep flows near a grassy bank. In the early fall the browns are especially willing to take the big mouse patterns. The opportunities are limited only by imagination and all of it is within a few minutes of my deck and that gas grill. Smear some butter on the surface of piece of tinfoil, put a little crushed garlic and some pepper on the inside of that brown trout, wrap it in the tinfoil and throw it on the grill. What could be better than having a fresh trout for dinner, especially if it is one caught on that same afternoon?

CHAPTER EIGHT

Ar-Kansas or Ar-Cansaw?— Flowing the Wrong Way

Just like any other river, the Arkansas can be fished when the water is high. The secret is to identify those places where trout will lurk below some cover, waiting for a morsel to drift by. When small islands are covered with water they create the perfect resting place. Note the plant barely above the water near the far bank. Chances are that your next catch is just below those grassy shoots.

I was actually born on the Eastern Slope, but my parents moved from my birthplace in Cripple Creek to Ouray when I was six months old. Both sides of my family are several generations deep in Colorado.

As a youngster I spent untold hours in the back seat of a car traveling from Ouray to Cripple Creek and Victor, with occasional trips to Canon City, Denver and Colorado Springs. I would gaze out the window at the various streams and beaver ponds beside the highway and try to visualize the trout, which I just knew were lurking there, just waiting for me to challenge them with a fly, or even a fat worm.

I cannot remember when I actually learned about the Continental Divide. It seems like I have always known that all the water on one side of Monarch Pass goes east and all the water on the other side goes west, at least in general terms. But I always had the sense that the rivers and streams on the east side of the divide flowed the wrong way. They seem to upset my natural sense of direction. The Arkansas River is one of those waters that sometimes seem to me to flow uphill.

I remember learning sometime in my past that the Arkansas River flows into the Mississippi River. It is rather exciting in my way of thinking to know that Huckleberry Finn may have floated on waters that started high in the mountains of Colorado. Before anyone gets too excited, I do know that Huckleberry is a fictional character, but never the less, a character that I have no problem identifying with. I also remember my fifth-grade teacher, Olive Brown, insisting that the name of the river should be pronounced, "Ar-Kansas," not "Ar-cansaw." I think it had something to do with a state law passed by the state of Arkansas, which required that the state name be pronounced with the "saw" at the end, but the name of the river did not fall under that same law. I argued the point with a number of people who mispronounced the river over the years, but I never prevailed, so I usually pronounce the name of the river the same as I pronounce the name of the state. It avoids conflict.

I first fished the Arkansas River with one of my cousins when I was in my mid-teens. We drove down the Phantom Canyon Road from Cripple Creek to Canon City and fished the river just above Canon City. Since then my fishing of the river has been limited to occasional stops during trips, which were generally being made for other reasons. I have an uncanny knack of mixing business with pleasure. I find that the practice makes business much easier to cope with.

More than one business trip required me to travel to Colorado Springs. Somehow my fly rod and fishing vest ends up stashed somewhere in whatever vehicle I might be driving. For many years I did not really plan to stop along the Arkansas River. My plans often included some of the small creeks I know along the way. But one thing led to another and during one of my trips I found myself traveling down the Arkansas Canyon. I was ahead of schedule and had made only one short fishing side trip only to be discouraged by some above average spring runoff. I noted that the Arkansas River was running high, but it was surprisingly clear. Since that trip I give much more attention to the Arkansas.

A high river does not necessarily mean it cannot be fished. With a little practice, one can learn to read the river and identify those little holes and eddies near the bank. Fish are no different from any other animal, including some of us human sorts. We all like to eat as much as possible without expending any more energy than necessary.

There are a number of good access points to the river below Salida, all part of the Arkansas Headwaters Recreation Area under the direction of the Colorado Parks and Wildlife. Most are well marked on the highway and the BLM has erected, "entering public lands" signs. Be aware, however, that these markings are not near as obvious if you are walking along the bank of the river.

My favorite spots are below Cotopaxi, beginning at the Texas Creek area. The spring runoff, as I said earlier, makes things a little challenging, but try some weighted nymph patterns and be very aware of those small slow moving areas up close to the bank and below any type of structure in the river. One of my favorite springtime flies is the beaded head stonefly, but this is another instance when I sometimes leave the fly rod in the case and pick up a good spinning rod. Throwing a fairly large Mepps or Rooster Tail spinner or a Daredevil spoon will very often yield those 12-14-inch rainbows and an occasional 16-inch brown. The entire area, as far as I know, is limited to flies and lures and has some catch-and-release rules. Be sure to check the regulations before taking a trip. They (CPW) have a nasty habit of changing them on a not-so-regular basis. In early 2014 CPW designated the Upper Arkansas as Gold Medal waters from the Lake Fork near Leadville downstream to Parkdale at the Highway 50 bridge crossing above the Royal Gorge.

My last stop on one of these trips is usually at the Five Points Recreation Area. The river has a small split there and provides some slower water. Because these "business trips" are often during the week, the fishing pressure is much lower than it might be on any given weekend. I am not promoting goofing off on company time, but everyone needs a break now and then. Funny thing is, I still get the feeling the river is running the wrong direction, but it is not near as obvious when I am standing knee-deep in the water. The fish still tend to face upstream regardless which side of the great Continental Divide they are on.

CHAPTER NINE

Crawford Reservoir— Just For the Fish of It

When Crawford Lake is low, it presents a challenge to the ice fisherman. Some scouting before the ice and snow sets in is often a good idea. Identifying rock beds and possible hiding places for the crappie and perch is easier without the winter cover.

If you have not figured it out by now, I will do everything I can in what follows to convince you that I do not conform very well to the typical fisherman that one might see on one of those television shows where the guest celebrity or the overpaid host hauls in one fish after another and then kisses it goodbye and returns it to the water.

I do not have a problem with catch-and-release fishing. I do it quite often and I think, in the right places and at the right times, it should be done, either by choice or by regulation. I return the overwhelming majority of the rainbow trout I catch to the water. Most rainbows in my opinion are rather bland tasting and I am better served by the catch-and-release practice. I do not freeze trout of any kind to eat later. When I catch a nice brown and I am in the mood for eating a nice brown, I keep it and eat it within a day or two of the catching. The same goes for native cutthroats.

As far as I am concerned, the walleye is about the best eating fish there is and, while my walleye catching opportunities are very limited; I am not beyond keeping a few of them when the opportunity arises.

That brings us to perch. Perch are about as close to walleye as any fish can be. Where they are available, they are usually plentiful and I catch them to eat them—period.

Yellow perch, more than any other thing is the reason I first started going to Crawford Reservoir. They are not the only reason that I go back frequently. Often I go for the crappie, which also holds a high place on my list of edible fish.

The Crawford Dam was among those projects, much like the Uncompahgre Project, that was not held as being very important in the early stages of the Colorado River Storage Project. The opponents of these "high elevation, low value" projects were very vocal in their opposition to the Smith Fork Project that created the Crawford Dam. But this was another of the projects, much like Ridgway, that garnered the attention of Congressman Wayne Aspinall. While the dam itself is on Iron Creek, the majority of the water comes from the Smith Fork of the Gunnison River, which is diverted by a smaller diversion dam and a canal in order to direct the water into the reservoir. Crawford Dam is located about one mile south of the town of Crawford and the water behind it is used to irrigate a few crops of corn and barley, but primarily feed crops like hay and alfalfa.

I think the promoters of the dam knew that it could be a highly used recreation area. When I was originally researching the project I noted with interest that one highlight of the 1963 dedication ceremony was a group of water-skiers performing various tricks while skimming across the surface of the lake. Because the ceremony took place in mid-April, I am guessing that the skiers did not spend a lot of time in the water. Not surprisingly, Aspinall was among the spectators. The area has since become a very popular recreation area under the direction and control of the Colorado Parks and Wildlife. There are several campgrounds ranging from tent sites to full hookup RV facilities. CPW maintains an office at the lake.

Most of the perch that I get out of Crawford range between six and nine inches long, with a few going to 11 inches. Most of them are the result of ice fishing, which I consider to be the best way to fish Crawford. I often joke that I go to Crawford, fish for four hours, filet for two hours and eat for 15 minutes. I probably use up a lot more calories getting out on the ice and preparing the catch than I gain by eating them, even if I fry them, which I usually do.

After the ice thickens and is safe, using an underwater camera and sonar equipment can reduce the number of holes you might have to drill. Those fall photographs are also very helpful.

I have learned a lot about ice fishing since my first experience on Vega Reservoir many years ago. First, you never catch fish from the first hole you drill, but after you drill it and abandon it, someone else will come along, use the same hole and catch a stringer full. Second, fish never bite when you are watching the end of your rod. They prefer to hit you bait when you have a Thermos bottle of coffee in one hand and a cup in the other with no convenient place to put either one. Third, it is impossible to tie a jig to the end of your line with your gloves on and it is not impossible to drop the last jig of any given color or style in such a way as to make it bounce into a hole and disappear into the depth with no line attached.

Crawford also has a population of northern pike, but I would not give you a plug nickel for all of them. They were illegally stocked into the lake by some "bait bucket biologists" and the CPW biologists have been trying to deal with them ever since. Izaak Walton (I told you that you would be hearing more from him) wrote back in 1653 that, "All pikes that live long prove chargeable to their keepers, because their life is maintained by the death of so many other fish, even those of their own kind . . ." He called the pike a "fresh water wolf."

That brings me to crappie, which is the other reason I go to Crawford. I do catch some crappie through the ice, but more often I go in the spring and early summer. I take my little pontoon boat and row myself out to the willow beds, if they are under water, or I search out the rocky areas where the crappie often hang out.

The Crawford crappie are not historically big and would likely be laughed at by most Arkansas or Missouri fishermen, but they taste good. I have learned that it works better to skin them rather than try to filet them. The filets are rather small.

Crawford is one of those places that I often go alone. When I am sitting on a chair on the frozen surface of the lake or perched on top of my one-man boat, I can take some time to ponder my great place in life. I would not take all the wealth in the world for the family and friends I have, but neither would I take a fortune in trade for my time in the outdoors. One of the things I am always grateful for is the fact that, unlike the people of Izaak Walton's world, I do not have to get the King's permission to go fishing in the King's waters. And, I do not have to conform to the pressure of being politically correct all the time. Sometimes I just eat the fish I catch.

Chapter Ten

Buckhorn Lakes—An Old Favorite

Buckhorn Lakes, owned by the City of Montrose, is one of my favorite destinations for a few hours of fishing and relaxation. While the road tends to be a little rough, the views and the tranquility of the settings are worth the trip.

I doubt that there have been more than a few years since I was a pre-teen that I have not visited Buckhorn Lakes, east of Colona. Even when I was living on the eastern plains of Colorado, our summer trips back to Ouray always included a trip to Buckhorn Lakes.

Buckhorn Lakes is owned and managed as a park by the City of Montrose. I am sure the water is much more important to them than the park. Located about 7 miles east of Colona and only a total of about 15 miles from my home, the spot is an ideal destination for a late afternoon, or even an early morning. It is good for a few hours or a few days.

As with many of my memories, I can recall fishing at the Buckhorns with my dad and an uncle on my mother's side of the family. There was a time when the lakes held some record-threatening brook trout. We always did well early in the spring and again late in the fall. The mid-summer trips were usually less productive, but enjoyable. The scenery is great, and there is always wildlife to observe. The wild flowers are abundant.

Buckhorn Lakes is one of those places I go just to get away from people, phones and computers for a few hours. I come back home rejuvenated and ready to tackle the problems at hand once again. Just looking back over the Uncompahgre Valley from near Buckhorn Lakes is enough in itself to remind me how insignificant we really are in the overall scheme of things. Watching the wildlife, observing the first of the wild flowers that have poked up from the bright green grass that was covered with snow only days before, gives me a sense of wellbeing. I truly feel connected with life. A couple of hours of fishing just make it that much better.

Maybe my style of therapy is not right for everyone. Frankly, I hope it isn't. There are some seriously sick people out there, many of which I would just as soon not meet at my local fishing hole, much less on a hunting trip. But for me it is just what I need every now and then and I know there a lot of people who could be helped if they would just buy a fishing license.

During my younger years it was not uncommon for a couple of my pals and me to con someone into taking us up to Buckhorn, dropping us off and coming back to get us two or three days later. Sometimes we would pitch a small tent or two, other times we simply curled up in sleeping bags next to the fire. While we took along some necessities for meals, it was a rare occasion that we did not have a few nice brook trout to supplement our menu.

Many years ago, while camping at the lakes, I was awakened by the sounds of a hammer and saw. At the time a man named Archie Runyon was the Montrose parks superintendent. As I recall, and my memory is admittedly a little foggy on this, Runyon was all alone that morning and was building an outhouse. I think he was responsible for a number of the improvements in the park, including picnic tables and fire pits. He died in 1996 and there is surprisingly little information about him. I do remember him as being a hard worker and a lover of the outdoors. My attempts to contact a relative were unsuccessful.

While some management practices that were wrong in my book greatly reduced the numbers of big brook trout over the years, there are indications that they are coming back and the stocking program has changed in a way that will help that happen.

By far the best way to fish either of the two Buckhorn Lakes is from a small boat either hand powered or with a small electric motor. I like my one-man pontoon boat for this purpose. Slowly moving around the lake, while paying close attention to the shoreline and the inlets, I like to pull a wooly bugger fly, allowing it to sink just below the surface. Casting a black doll fly often has the same results and gets down to the where the late summer fish hang out.

Another very effective method, when a boat is not available is the use of a fly and bubble rig using a spinning rod and reel. Mosquitoes are popular, both as fishing lures and as pests, so take along some repellent.

Not far above and to the east of Buckhorn Lakes is another lake that requires a little hike, but Onion Lake can be worth the trip. The lake shows up on most topo maps. That fly and bubble method is exceptionally useful at the Onion.

CHAPTER ELEVEN

South Fork of Mineral Creek— Ignoring the Crowd

A fishing trip into the South Mineral drainage is enhanced by a side-trip to Clear Lake. An ATV is the optimum transportation for the trip, but any good 4WD will suffice. The view of the valley from the Clear Lake road is amazing.

In those formative years, when I roamed the streets of Ouray and caused as much grief as I could to some of the people that I should have paid more attention to, I always found comfort in the fact that a hunting or fishing trip was never too far away.

I must confess that many of my trips were made without the express consent of my parents and I often associated with people much older than me because they offered me the chance to do things that older people do. My friends and I were nothing if we were not resourceful. We learned how to convince people to give us a lift long before we had driver's licenses and many of us experimented with driving before we were legally supposed to be behind the wheel. We literally learned to drive on the famous Million Dollar Highway, between Ouray and Silverton.

Back then a trip to the South Fork of Mineral Creek, better known simply as South Mineral, rarely meant dealing with a lot of people. We could literally walk up the South Mineral road and step off into the stream to catch those prize little brook trout.

Mineral Creek itself begins somewhere near the Ouray/San Juan County line near Red Mountain Pass. As it flows down through the canyon, it gathers more water, from Mill Creek, which comes out of Columbine Lake, then the Middle Fork that headwaters just south of Ophir Pass, and then its biggest tributary, The South Fork. South Mineral finds it origin on the sides of peaks that jut up to well over 13,000 feet, somewhere between Rolling Mountain and Twin Sisters. The terrain is largely rock with very little light dirt, which makes the creek flow almost crystal clear most of the time. It is one of those streams that are better fished while going upstream so the fish can be approached from behind. It is necessary, when fishing South Mineral or any similar water, to be quiet. Slow movements, whether in or out of the water, will more often pay off than sloshing around in the faster moving water or tromping up and down the banks. There are numerous beaver ponds, but they are for the most part shallow and need to be approached with a certain amount of stealth.

The best time to fish South Mineral is before anyone else walks or wades the area on any given day. That has become a problem. For some reason, largely the accessibility I think, South Mineral is very popular. It is a rare summer weekend that the South Mineral campground is not full and there are usually a good number of small tents pitched along the creek below the campground. There are not as many above there, but certainly enough.

An interesting thing is that most of these outdoor enthusiasts are not there for the fishing. Most of them come for the hiking, and there is ample opportunity for that. One thing that seems to be more and more common though are those who have no idea what mining and mining claims are. Some think that because there are no signs and no equipment around a mine it gives them the right to wander all over the claim and pick up, or even dig for whatever specimen or artifact they might find.

During one trip I engaged in a conversation with a couple who were actively digging into the dump at the Bandora Mine, which is a couple of miles above the campground. It turns out that the man determined through an Internet search that Chalcopyrite, reportedly from the Bandora, was being sold on EBay and was bringing in a tidy sum. It was very obviously distressing, judging by this guy's language, that he did not like me telling him that those specimens being sold on EBay were technically stolen property if they were being removed from a legal mining claim, which I am sure the Bandora is. All of San Juan and Ouray Counties are home to a plethora of mining claims. Many of them are patented, meaning they technically qualify as real estate, giving the owners both surface and mineral rights. Digging, entering tunnels or messing around any equipment is both dangerous and illegal, not to mention being immoral.

Back to fishing: First, I mentioned earlier the problem with lots of people. A lot of people around do not mean the fishing is going to be bad. In fact, it seems as though having all those people walking up and down the creek sometimes causes the trout to be less wary. The fact that not all of those people are fishing is a good thing. It makes some of the common offerings more acceptable to the trout.

For the fly fishing enthusiast, I recommend using a light rod and very light tackle. Keep with the small tippets and use small flies. Hoppers, Adams and blue-winged olive patterns are usually good choices, as are the dry attractors. Here, again, don't overlook the opportunity to use some spin-cast gear. The small spinners will often work when flies do not. They will bring those stubborn brookies out from under the bank. Use one of the popular ultra-light rods with 2-pound test line, but try to fish upstream. These tasty little spotted fish in South Mineral are rarely bigger than 10 inches. They are very prolific, spawning in the fall and often over populate some of the high mountain streams. Even the most ardent catch-and-release folks often agree that keeping a limit of brookies for supper is a good idea.

There are other fishing options during a trip to South Mineral. A good 4WD, or better yet, an ATV makes a drive to Clear Lake a cinch. The road forks off of the South Mineral Creek road just below the campground. Clear Lake offers some quality high mountain lake fishing and certainly some great scenery. Don't leave the camera behind.

Another choice is to take the hike up to Ice Lake. Plan on encountering more than a few people on this hike, but there are usually more walking sticks than fly rods and damn few fat old men.

CHAPTER TWELVE

Crystal River—A Trout and Mountain Whitefish Opportunity

A lot has been said and written about the Roaring Fork River, but the Crystal River, which is a tributary of the Roaring Fork, can be every bit as much fun to fish and often without the crowds. The Crystal holds one of the best populations of mountain white fish found in Colorado.

As Colorado mountain passes go, McClure Pass does not rate among the lofty ones. Cresting at 8,755 feet above sea level, the pass comes in at 35th place on the Colorado Department of Transportation's list of passes. But, being high and mighty is not the only attribute to a beautiful and historical Colorado drive, especially if the reason for the drive is another fishing trip.

The few times I traversed over McClure Pass during my youth I remember it as being mostly dirt road with a lot of rocks. By 1978, some two years before I moved back to Western Colorado, the highway was paved, but it still has a lot of rocks. Highway 133 has a long interesting history, but as it is today, it stretches from

Highway 92 at Hotchkiss to Highway 182 at Carbondale, roughly 71 miles. The road above Paonia traverses along the Paonia Reservoir, a body of water that has never been a great fishery. The reservoir is another of the side projects of the Colorado River Storage Project and was completed in early 1962, after being in the planning and budgeting process for many years. The lake is subject to a large amount of silt and was illegally stocked with northern pike years ago. The Colorado Parks and Wildlife took advantage of the low water in 2013, killed off the pike population and started stocking the lake with rainbows. It will stay as a low priority on my fishing list.

At the bottom of the east side of McClure, Highway 133 pretty much follows the route of the Crystal River, which flows through what was once called the Valley of the Coal Miners. The River's origin is in the Elk Mountains above Marble. The word "crystal" is a commonly used descriptive in Colorado. I have no idea how many Crystal Lakes and Crystal Creeks there are in the state, but Crystal River certainly deserves the name. I have rarely seen the river muddy or even slightly turbid. It routinely flows crystal clear.

Some great fishing opportunities exist along the river on Gunnison County Road 3 above Marble, but be advised that this is not a road for your daddy's Oldsmobile. It is best travelled on an ATV, and at the rate our government is closing roads, be sure to check if even that is allowed before planning a trip. Below Marble there are many places to fish the river, but again, there is a lot of private property that must be respected. When in doubt, ask one more question.

I have heard for years that as soon as it starts getting hot trout stop going after stonefly patterns. Hogwash. I do not buy into the idea that trout have calendars and watches. They are opportunity feeders. If they are looking for food and you give them something that looks good to eat, you catch them.

Often fly fishers associate the stonefly with nymph fishing. That is good. The stonefly nymph is typically rather large and provides a substantial part of a trout's food requirements during a time when they need it, especially the spawn-age trout. The adult stonefly is a nice mouthful for any trout. The females do not swarm when they are laying eggs. They often rest on top of the water and flutter while laying. This action explains why a trout will take an adult stonefly pattern at about any time, but if the stoneflies are actually present in the ecosystem at the time, you have an even better chance of getting that hungry old trout. Those adult stoneflies, tied on rather large hooks, have always been good choices for me on the Crystal.

But, there is another opportunity on the Crystal, one that not all that many people are aware of. The mountain whitefish is one of only two salmonids that are native to Colorado. When the whitefish is mentioned among fishing enthusiasts, most recall the days when the whitefish was so prominent in the Yampa River drainage in northwestern Colorado, and many of those people consider the fish to be somewhat of a trash fish. Regardless, they are fun to catch and there is a respectable population of them in the Crystal River. My early trips to the area were made specifically to go after the whitefish.

Whitefish are tough. They can survive some very extreme temperature changes and are not as likely to succumb to those changes, as are some of the introduced species, although there is information that whirling disease hit the Colorado mountain whitefish rather heavily during the disease's peak in the late 1990s.

While I generally return my whitefish to the water now, there was a time when I did not. I think the first smoked fish I ever ate was a whitefish caught in the Crystal River.

You can catch whitefish with much the same techniques as those to catch trout, but the smaller fly patterns, in particular nymphs, have always been good for me. My favorite list for the Crystal River includes Royal Wulffs, Caddis, Stoneflies, in both nymph and adult patterns and Hare's Ears. Most of the nymphs I use are on a size 14 or smaller. A dropper fly seems to work better if it is on the long side.

Colorado fishermen will hear a lot about the Roaring Fork River, but this much smaller river that feeds into the Roaring Fork is often a good option. There are some deep pools, nice shallow riffles and some great scenery.

CHAPTER THIRTEEN

Bonny Dam—Good Memories of a Place Now Gone

At one time Bonny Reservoir was a gem in the plains of Eastern Colorado. It is only a mud flat now. The Republican River nearly dried up over the years and the legalities of water compacts dictated that, rather than store any of the Republican water, it had to flow on to the lower states.

It is almost unfair for me to record here a place to go fishing that does not even exist. At least it no longer exists, but it deserves mention, if for no other reason than to record its former existence.

For someone who grew up looking at mountains in every direction, hiking into high mountain lakes and hunting elk, the eastern plains of Colorado came as somewhat of a shock. A year and a half after graduating from high school I found myself setting up housekeeping and starting a family in Burlington, Colorado.

My first impression of the area was that of a desolate flat land where the wind blew constantly and the highest things around were grain elevators and water towers. Then I discovered Bonny Dam.

The Flood Control Acts of 1944 and 1946 authorized the construction of Bonny Dam. Construction began in December of 1948 and was completed in May of 1951. While the primary purpose of the dam and the resulting lake was to control flooding of the Republican River, the project resulted in untold recreational opportunities. The lake quickly became a popular fishing and boating destination. People from Colorado Springs and Denver were frequent visitors.

Within weeks of moving to Burlington, I discovered the fun of waterfowl hunting at Bonny State Park and Bonny Lake. The area is located in Yuma County, about 24 miles north of Burlington. It was not unusual for some fellow workers and I to go duck hunting in the morning before work and clean the ducks in the back of the shop after returning for a day's work. I also learned that some of the best tasting fish I had ever had was the walleye caught from Bonny Lake.

I recall one of my first fishing trips to Bonny with some new friends. Our quarry for the trip was crappie, and a small weighted jig was working well when fished under a float. I decided to try using a fly rod with one of the jigs. To a man, everyone who observed my behavior thought I was suffering from some sort of identity crisis. This was long before fly fishing was popular for much of anything other than small trout, and there were no trout in Bonny.

A few minutes later, after I had landed half a dozen one-pound crappies, they began to look at my nine-foot piece of bamboo with some envy. I was having a great time.

While trolling was the preferred method of taking walleye, we also spent many nights fishing from the bank with night crawlers. That was also a good time to hook a catfish or two. The lake also produced bass in addition to the crappie, walleye and catfish, and it contained some of the largest carp I have ever seen along with a few drum. Later, the lake was stocked with wipers. Well-known walleye tournament champion Ron Seelhoff brags that he caught his first walleye from the waters of Bonny Dam when he was five years old. In 1973, Seelhoff participated in the annual Knights of Columbus fishing tournament. The competition sparked a desire in him and he went on to win numerous tournaments and trophies.

About a mile below the dam is the small village of Hale and the Hale ponds. The ponds were a great resource for bluegill and small mouth bass, and they were the base of operation for the annual Huck Finn Derby. My kids were introduced to fishing at the Hale Ponds.

In June of 2007 I had an opportunity to make a quick trip back to the Burlington area. Some of my first inquiries were focused on the fishing at Bonny Lake. Much to my disappointment, I learned that the lake was very low, almost 20 feet below the full mark and was holding only 31 per cent of its capacity. Launching anything other than small boats, according to the local experts, is almost impossible. The Republican River, which is the main water source for the lake, was nearly dry most of the time.

While the Flood Control Act was designed to slow the flow of the Republican River, it was necessary for Colorado to also comply with the Republican River Compact of 1942. In 1998 the State of Kansas filed a complaint to the United States District Court and alleged that Nebraska was not fulfilling the necessary requirements of allowing water to flow into Kansas, Colorado ended up involved in the suit because the Republican River was party to the compact. Most of the allegations involved the pumping of irrigation water, which the suit alleged caused less ground water flowing through Kansas and Nebraska. By the middle of 2002 the fate of Bonny Dam was sealed. It was totally drained a few years later and the popular Bonny State Park became a wildlife area.

I often relate that Bonny Dam helped maintain my sanity during those years in Kit Carson County. I never did get to where I liked the geography of that area, but the people are second to none. They are hardworking, dedicated individuals that will quite literally give anyone the shirt off their backs. I developed friendships that I will always treasure, many of them while fishing or shooting ducks at Bonny Dam.

CHAPTER FOURTEEN

Olathe Reservoirs— Meeting Nice People

The Olathe Reservoirs are nestled at the edge of Dry Creek Basin west of Montrose. The unusual fishery provides some great get-away time and always has the possibility of being a place to meet some really nice people.

There are not a lot of fishing opportunities nestled in among the piñon and juniper trees of Western Colorado. For the most part the land is arid with a small stream or two meandering through. Many of those streams have high alkali content and are not subject to being fish friendly. There are exceptions.

At the edge of the Dry Creek Basin west of Montrose the various tributaries of Dry Creek are trapped in a few lonely spots, among them the Olathe Reservoirs. I have to confess that I am not a frequent visitor to the reservoirs, but every time I travel into the bottom of that canyon, I come out with a story to tell.

The area around the Olathe Reservoirs is a perfect example of why ATVs are versatile toys. Many of the trips I took into the area were done trying to stay in the seat of a Jeep or similar 4-wheel drive contrivance. The road is rough and narrow, although not what I would call particularly dangerous. It is almost like opening a door into a glorious room when you drive through the willows near the number two reservoir and the small lake spreads out before you. It truly looks out of place among the adobe, piñon and juniper that surrounds it. It has the beauty of a high mountain lake, but is less than 8,000 feet above sea level.

There are rarely very many people at the Olathe Reservoirs and they are usually locals that love to talk about the area. I recall one trip in 2013 when I encountered a very special man.

When I arrived at the lake he was the only other person there. His ATV was parked on the shore and he was obviously enjoying the day. I almost felt guilty interrupting him. I regret now not asking him for his name.

Anyone who has been fishing for more than a day or two has encountered those people who are just plain nasty. They elbow their way into your comfort zone and don't even have the presence of mind to say, "Excuse me." They talk loud, throw things in the water for their dogs and leave a pile of trash behind. They usually have a couple of kids with them that are quickly learning the art of being obnoxious.

So, here I was driving up behind the only other fisherman at the lake and interrupting him. Like I said, I was feeling a little guilty, but we struck up a conversation and he told me how long he had been there, how many fish he caught and what he was using to catch them. Then came a question I have never heard anyone ask.

This gentleman looked me square in the eye and said, "I bet I am in your favorite spot." When I told him that I really did not have a favorite spot and explained that it had been years since I had fished the lake. He said, "Well this is a pretty good spot. I'll move if you want to try it here for awhile."

Why would a man give up a good fishing spot to someone he never met before? The answer is simple and yet complicated: This man has manners. I am betting that he opens doors for the ladies and takes his hat off when he enters a home. I am betting that he thanks people for what they do and I am betting that he grew up respecting his elders. I am betting that he had a mentor of some kind years ago that took him fishing and didn't just tell him how to treat others, but rather showed him how to treat others. I am betting that, while I do not know this man at all, I am completely accurate in calling him a gentleman.

I went to the far side of the lake and fished for a couple of hours and brought home enough for supper that night. The natives were rich, pink meat specimens that went well with some homemade soup. The fish satisfied my hunger, not that I often go hungry, but my short encounter with another man satisfied much more than the physical hunger.

Now, the next time I meet one of those obnoxious human beings that either never had the mentoring they needed or did not pay attention to it, I will think of that nice guy that I met at the Olathe Reservoir. I may never know his name, but he will always be a gentleman in my book. He proved to me that you meet the nicest people where they are, and they are everywhere, just waiting to meet someone else that has manners.

Getting to the Olathe Reservoirs is relatively easy, but a whole day should be dedicated to the trip. Leave Montrose to the west on Highway 90 and follow that route until you reach the edge of Dry Creek. At this point the Rim Road traverses along the rim of the Dry Creek Canyon. Turn north on Rim Road and drive a little over three miles to where the road intersects with the small road that drops into the bottom of the canyon, cutting back to the south. This is a good place unload your ATV. It is probably another three miles to the lower lake, which I think is the best fishing.

As for tackle, again I go with the smaller spinners and I prefer to use a fly and bubble combination. That means I have to bring in a lot less gear. One good spinning rod is usually enough. This is one of those places I go to get some eating fish. Typically, I catch native cutthroats, with a few brookies. I only keep enough for one or two meals.

CHAPTER FIFTEEN

East Dallas Creek— The Formative Years

A line of willows along the edges of East Dallas Creek gave rise to the name, Willow Swamp. While not being a truly prolific habitat for a lot of fish, it is regularly stocked and makes for some great fishing.

If any locale in Colorado is responsible for my becoming so appreciative of the outdoors, it has to be the East Dallas Creek drainage. East Dallas Creek has its beginnings at the very base of Mount Sneffels and the Blue Lakes. It tumbles, first through a rocky canyon, then slows through a beautiful miniature valley loaded with willows, and then starts another plunge from an altitude of about 9,300 feet to where it dumps into Dallas Creek at about 7,000 feet.

On the way down, East Dallas takes on the water from the much smaller Beaver Creek. Beaver Creek is for the most part on private land and is not really practical to fish, but that was not always so. When I was about five years old, my dad took me fishing on Beaver Creek. I remember the approximate date because we slept in a relatively new 1955 Desoto that night. Dad curled up in the front seat and I had the massive back seat to myself. I later wondered why the roles were not switched, but I guess that is the way fathers are.

What was most important was that I caught my very first fish from that little creek, using a willow pole, about six feet of line, a hook with a small split-shot sinker and a wiggling worm. That was also the first time I ate brook trout within eyesight of where I caught them. I still have a frying pan and some cornmeal handy for those kinds of trips. Every time I drive up East Dallas Road I slow down as I drive over the culvert that allows Beaver Creek to cross under the road. I always have a sense of frying fish and a warm quilt and remember that my dad took the time and patience to show me how to fish.

A few miles upstream from Beaver Creek, the East Dallas meanders through a small valley, which has been named Willow Swamp. It is not really a swamp, but rather a place where the water takes a rest and provides the local beavers with the opportunity to dam up parts of the stream and make their homes. One beaver pond has become somewhat permanent over the years. It is shallow, as many beaver ponds are, but still offers some fishing opportunity if approached carefully. I had to laugh when I read the account of one of those self-appointed experts on the area. He or she (they artfully leave out their names on a lot of this garbage) described this beaver pond as being "East Dallas Lake." I have been around the area a long time and know most of the past and present landowners of the area. I know of no other person who thinks there is a "lake" in Willow Swamp.

Willow Swamp does offer some good fishing. I prefer to go there in the spring before the water is too high and before the droves of stick-walkers head up the Blue Lakes Trail, but getting all the way to the campground is usually a 4WD proposition and I have more than once been discouraged by a large snowdrift just beyond the forest boundary. Every year is different, but heavy snowfall can keep the road impassible until early June.

Since I mentioned Blue Lakes, I should probably follow up. Just above Willow Swamp is the trailhead to Blue Lakes. The Blue Lakes Trail is one of the more popular trails in the San Juan Mountains. Much like the Highland Mary Trail mentioned earlier, primarily people that just want to hike from point A to point B use the trail. I don't understand it, but that is what they do. A few of them carry a fly rod and wear a hat that cost $100, but most of them just hike. Their goal is to get to the top, turn around and come back.

The Blue Lakes can be accessed via the Dallas side or the more challenging Ouray side above Yankee Boy Basin. Either way, the hike is steep. I admit that I used the Yankee Boy route only once and that was when I was young and had healthy knee joints. I have walked up the Dallas side several times and hope to do it once more before I become entirely too decrepit. Keep in mind that, in less than five miles you are going to go from about 9,300 feet to near 11,000 feet in elevation. The trail has some great switchbacks that will remind you on a regular basis how fast you are gaining altitude.

I fished in the upper two lakes only once, and that was on that trip we took from the Yankee Boy side. The lower lake, which is the first one encountered on the trail from the East Dallas, has always been good to me, but it is like any other high mountain lake. When it is good it is really good and when it is bad you catch nothing.

I know that the modern fly-fishing crowd probably cringes when I say it, but using a fly and bubble rig is about the best way to fish this lake. It is fun to cast a fly when Mother Nature provides just the right cloud cover and the lake has a mirror finish, but I am not the best long-range fly caster. My fly-fishing is better served in small streams or rivers where I can reach my quarry with a well-placed roll cast. Take the fly rod and wear the $100 hat, but don't discount the spinning tackle.

The other thing, and I do not mention it enough, is be sure to take a camera. This area provides some of the best scenery you can imagine and it has the potential of providing memories that you will cherish for years. I know I do.

CHAPTER SIXTEEN

The Big Cimarron—A Week's Vacation

The Big Cimarron River is never really big. As it flows through the ranchland in the lower valleys it shows little of the grandeur of its upper reaches where the East Fork, Middle Fork and West Fork come together. The three main tributaries along with the limited availability in the lower reaches can be a great excuse to take a week off and go fishing.

The Big Cimarron River and the drainages associated with it certainly fall within my favorite places in Western Colorado. If the East Dallas area molded me for the appreciation of the outdoors, the Cimarron certainly refined that appreciation.

The water of the Big Cimarron River comes from the three forks of that river, namely the East Fork, the Middle Fork and the West Fork. The headwaters of all three forks are on the sides of some of the most beautiful and most visited high peaks of the San Juans. Precipice Peak (13,144), Redcliff (13,642), Coxcomb

Peak (13,656), Wetterhorn Peak (14,017) and Uncompahgre Peak (14,309) all form huge panoramic basins, rich in all types of alpine flora. They are all coveted destinations for mountain climbers, hikers and photographers, and of course, us lowly fishermen.

The drainages encompass parts of Ouray, Hinsdale and Gunnison Counties. It is not an area that can even be closely appreciated in a day or two, or for that matter a lifetime, but it is a great choice for a week's vacation.

When I have visitors from outside the area, and I want to show off the splendor of the place in which I live, I almost always choose a drive over Owl Creek Pass. Beginning on the Big Cimarron Road at the intersection with U.S. Highway 50 about 24 miles east of Montrose, you can traverse over Owl Creek and ultimately get back to paved road when Ouray County Road 10 intersects with U.S. 550 about two miles north of Ridgway. The circle back to Montrose ends in an 85-mile-long trip that has the possibilities of not only great scenery but an abundance of wildlife. I have observed everything from ground squirrels to an occasional moose and everything from the smallest songbirds to turkeys. And, of course there is the fishing.

My favorite way to enjoy the Cimarron country is to park a camp trailer near the confluence of the East and Middle Forks or in the Silver Jack campground. Unfortunately, some of the great thinkers in the U.S. Forest Service choose to close the campground after Labor Day, leaving some of the best times of the year without its benefits. There are no hook-ups there, but it is convenient and the pads are level.

This is great ATV country and most of the roads are open to their use. Dedicating a day to each of the forks is not a hard thing to do. The area may look somewhat crowded, but the users are as diversified as I have encountered anywhere. There are hikers and bikers, walkers and stalkers (game stalkers), and even a significant number of people who just set up camp and lounge around the campfire. It is almost impossible to take a bad picture of the area, so cameras are everywhere. Surprisingly, with a few exceptions I will note later, there are usually not that many people fishing.

All three of the forks are subject to spring flooding and the path of the creeks will change dramatically from one season to the next. The prominent fish is the native cutthroat. Do not plan on wall-hangers, but I have latched on to a 16-inch fighter now and then. These streams are the perfect place for my type of fly-fishing. There is little need for those long, crowd-pleasing casts. In fact, a simple roll-cast is often the best approach. The water, except in the early spring, is almost always very clear, so work upstream whenever possible and walk around those special places where you need to go downstream. Drift your fly from as far upstream as possible in these situations.

It takes little more than a shadow or a splash to send these wary fish back into hiding for the rest of the day.

Small flies and nymphs are my choices. Sure, if there is a new hatch, you should try to match it, but the name of the fly is not, in my opinion, as important as a lot of people would like to make you think. I take my time, partly because it is good fishing strategy, but mostly because my worn out knee joints complain a lot about the round rocks that I have to stumble over. I find the use of a walking stick to be very beneficial.

Cutthroats, like brook trout are harder to spot in the water than are rainbows and they are always aware of things that like to eat them, like eagles, hawks, mink and people. Avoid moving in quick motions (like tripping on a rock) and plan well ahead of where you are. Look upstream for those special places that hold trout and try not to throw your casts in a manner in which the line will fall on what could be a future cast. I like to work close, and then make each cast to an area a little farther upstream. Using a "high stick" will keep as much line as possible off of the surface of the water during the drift. Casting to the same place more than once rarely nets a fish.

After spending two or three days fishing the three forks of the Cimarron, it is time to relax a little. Just below the confluence of the East Fork and Middle Fork, the waters flow into Silver Jack Reservoir, which is another of the multitude of water projects on the Western Slope that was constructed by the United States Bureau of Reclamation. It was completed in 1971 and has a maximum capacity of almost 13,000 acre-feet of water. Access is rather limited but non-motorized boats are permitted.

The first time I saw Silver Jack it scared the heck out of me. The spillway is known as a "morning glory" spillway. It amounts to a huge cone that somewhat resembles the flower it is named after sticking up out of the water. When the lake reaches capacity, it simply overflows into this big drain. It was working well on the day I was there, and you couldn't pay me enough to put a boat anywhere near it. Of course, there are safety measures in place, but it is still an impressive sight.

The fishing in Silver Jack is okay, but after those days of walking the creeks, I am ready to walk slowly on relative flat land and maybe even sit down for a while. Beaver Lake, located below Silver Jack is not fed by the Big Cimarron. The water comes from various smaller tributaries and the lake is a beautiful small lake that is well suited for relaxing. The lake has become very popular over the past several years, so you will not be alone, but timing is everything. I like spring and fall.

Beaver Lake, which is below the confluences of the various forks of the Cimarron River and below Silver Jack Reservoir is a perfect example of fishing close to the bank. Historically, Beaver Lake has given up some impressive sized brook trout. It is regularly stocked and nearby camping areas makes it a popular place for locals and tourist alike.

The title of this book owes a lot to Beaver Lake. It is the first place I remember learning the lesson that casting out to the middle of the lake is not always necessary, just as it is not necessary to travel great distances to have great experiences. The biggest fish I took out of Beaver Lake came from right under the bank of the west side of the lake. Because of the fishing pressure and the practice of regular stocking of the lake, rainbows are common, with an occasional brown or brook.

Above Beaver Lake, just across from the Silver Jack Overlook, is the road to another of my favorite spots, Rowdy Lake. While the road is appropriate for any 4WD, this is another road where an ATV is ideal. Here, your Royal Coachman fly or your Adams can net you some impressive native cutthroats that eat very well back at camp. If you still have a little walk left in you, follow the trail that begins at the north end of Rowdy and walk up to Clear Lake and Clear Lake II. The walk is worth the tranquil setting of these ponds and the fishing is usually fair, again the cutthroats are the name of the game.

That will pretty much take care of a week in the Big Cimarron, but mark my words, as soon as you leave the area you will be planning a return trip.

CHAPTER SEVENTEEN

Blue Mesa Lake and the Water Below—Deep Memories

There is probably not a fisherman alive that knows anything about Colorado who doesn't know about Blue Mesa Reservoir. Being the largest body of water in Colorado means that the best way to take advantage of the rainbows, browns, kokanee and lake trout is to skim the surface with a boat, but alternatives do exist.

During 1962 and much of 1963, due to bad health and the ultimate death of my grandmother, my dad and I made frequent trips from Ouray to Cripple Creek. Early in 1962 construction began on the Blue Mesa dam and reservoir project. The construction of the dam and the supporting road system was in full swing during the summer and autumn of 1962. Almost weekly, we could see the progress of the dam and the bridges. We could observe the "high scalers" on the cliffs and the grouters plying their trade.

While much of the country anticipated the filling of Blue Mesa for its water storage, I looked at it as a giant fishing pond.

It was exciting for me to know that less than 100 miles from my home would be the largest body of water in Colorado. How many fish could live in a lake that is 20 miles long? While I had some misgivings about losing some of the river fishing, especially near the old Sapinero Bridge, I could not help but be excited over the prospect of such a large lake.

No sooner did the lake fill with water, than I started making frequent trips. I quickly found that access without a boat was limited. When I moved back to the area after being gone for 10 years, one of the first things I did was buy a boat. Since then I have fished just about every nook and cranny of Blue Mesa. I have fished through the ice and from a boat. I have walked miles up the lake fork and camped on the shores.

The lake has evolved into the largest kokanee fishery in the United States, and is rated at the top of places to catch trophy-sized mackinaws. A good-sized chunk of sucker meat proved to be one of the best baits for those big macs. Most serious fishermen have also found that a downrigger is a good investment, as is a fish-finder and a GPS unit.

I no longer own a boat, but have occasionally gone with friends or rented one of the pontoon boats from the marina. That way, they pay for the permits and I don't have to store the boat or figure out why the outboard motor will not start. I also like to take early spring trips and fish from the bank.

The fishing below Blue Mesa Dam is a challenge but one that is worth the effort. The first access is accomplished by going down the Pine Creek Trail. Actually, the trail is not a trail at all. It is a succession of 232 stairs built out of various combinations of wood, rock and concrete, and dropping a couple of hundred feet into the canyon. The trail continues along the south side of the river to a boat dock used by the National Parks Service. It is a great hike whether the fishing is good or not. Kokanee snagging below Blue Mesa Reservoir has historically opened on September 1, but be sure and check the regulations before you take my word for it.

If the kokanee are not running, or if the timing is a little off, do not fret. There are some tremendous fish lurking in the waters between the Blue Mesa Dam and the stilling waters of

Morrow Point. Large streamer flies are often productive and, depending on the time of the year, mayfly patterns are great, as are the various stoneflies. Big flashy spoons work well on most days and the larger buck-tailed spinners are good choices. Pay attention to those large rocks along the bank.

Below the Morrow Point Dam is the Crystal Dam, the third and last in this group of dams designed for storing water and providing hydroelectric power. Crystal Reservoir is an adventure just waiting to happen.

Mid March is a dangerous time of the year for me. Living as I do in the lower part of a valley, I sometimes tend to forget that just minutes away from my house it is still winter. On any given day we can have warming sunshine or whiteout blizzards. We can wake up to beautiful blue skies or we can shovel our way out to where the newspaper delivery person threw the paper in a pile of fresh snow. We can plan a fishing trip or spend the day locked up inside the house feeding wood into the stove.

Below Morrow Point Dam where the Cimarron River dumps into the Gunnison River one may, with a little courage and desire, launch a small boat and float downstream onto the lake behind Crystal Dam. There is always the prospect of an adventure hidden in a day's fishing on Crystal.

For several years some friends and I would venture into the Black Canyon below Morrow Point Dam onto the waters behind Crystal Dam. We made this crazy trip on St. Patrick's Day. I must warn you that this trip is not for the fainthearted. I have long since given in to the extra few inches and pounds and allowed the tradition to fade, but in years past, four to six of us would get together. We would take two or three 12-foot aluminum boats to the Gunnison River, just below Morrow Point Dam at the confluence of the Cimarron River. There is no direct access to the river, so the boats would have to be carried, or in some cases skidded across the snow to the river. We then mounted the motors, loaded our gear, and started downstream. With over 400 feet of concrete dam looming behind us, we would navigate the river down onto the still water created by Crystal Dam. Then the fishing began.

Each year brought new challenges. Snow and ice routinely fell from the cliffs above. Often full-fledged avalanches roared down the side canyons, dumping a few hundred tons of snow into the calm waters and creating a miniature tidal wave. Often the lake was only partially thawed. Drifting ice once trapped us in a small cove, and we learned that 12-foot fishing boats do not function well as icebreakers.

The fishing was great. That is not to say that the catching was always good. When we did get fish, they were usually rainbows weighing in at two or three pounds each. Big red and white spoons tied to a spinning rod, or big ugly flies with sinking line on an eight-foot fly rod always worked well.

After several hours of camaraderie and colossal fishing, it was time to head back upriver. Usually the time coincided with a sudden rush of mud coming down the Cimarron River or an unscheduled release of water from Morrow Point that would cause the level of the river to rise just above a number of large boulders, each of which lay in wait to ding a propeller, take out a shear pin, and send you floating aimlessly back down the river. Oh to have had an airboat!

The Black Canyon, part of which is filled with the water behind the Crystal Dam, is a mind expanding exhibit of Precambrian, metamorphic and igneous rock that towers above the lake. Birds of prey routinely dive into the crevices and soar to the rims. The beauty and awe of the surroundings is reason enough to make the trip. The fish are but extra benefits given to those of us who are lucky enough to find the right combinations.

Should you decide to venture into this realm, let me give you some advice: First, take plenty of warm clothing. Dress in layers. Take life jackets, and wear them. Take some extra gas for the boat motor, and a pocketful of shear pins. Above all, enjoy yourself. And take pictures. I took very few during those years and now have only my memory to depend on.

CHAPTER EIGHTEEN

Black Canyon and the Gunnison Gorge—Deep and Inviting

The road down into the Black Canyon and the East Portal of the Gunnison River was greatly improved to accommodate the construction of Crystal Dam. The dam was completed in 1976. The road is still steep and is closed during the winter months, but the fishing below the dam and on below into the Black Canyon can be some of the finest found in Colorado.

Over the years I have fished the Gunnison River at many locations and, as a young man, traversed many of the trails into the canyon, including Bobcat, Chukar, Duncan and Ute and I have been lucky enough to have some great fishing.

As far as I can remember, the first time I went into the depths of the Black Canyon was when I was about seven years old.

A friend of ours had a Dodge Power Wagon, which he had purchased as war surplus about 1956 or so. Four-wheel-drive vehicles were not real popular or common then. With the exception of a few jeeps, also of war surplus quality, there were very few 4wd vehicles around, even in Ouray. That made Bill's Dodge Power Wagon, which he called a "command car," somewhat of a novelty, and getting to ride in it, especially when the top was off, was a treat.

Long before Crystal Dam was a reality, the road off the south side of the Black Canyon to the East Portal of the Gunnison Tunnel was an adventure to travel, particularly for a bunch of kids, the oldest of which was only about 11 at the time. Bill loaded the bulk of two families up into that old Power Wagon, put it into low range, and slowly descended into the canyon. Once there, we would spread out along the river above the diversion dam and start drifting big worms down into the eddies and near the banks. I don't think I caught too many fish. I certainly don't specifically remember any, but I do remember Bill and his wife, Jean catching some really nice trout. We would eat a picnic lunch and head back up the road at an even slower speed.

That old Power Wagon groaned and groaned all the way out of the canyon at a pace not much faster than most people can walk. We may as well have been on an African safari. It was a true adventure, and I have never forgotten it.

My next trips down the East Portal road were much later. I was about 16 or 17 and had a 1951 Chevrolet Suburban that was a retired Ridgway school bus. It too, came out of the canyon at a snail's pace in 'granny gear.' I do remember fishing on those trips and I remember we caught some nice trout.

There were several of those trips before Crystal Dam was completed, and many more since. I still venture down the road, which is now paved and much improved since that 1956 trip.

Much of the fishing I did on the lower part of the Gunnison was done prior to the designation of Gold Medal Waters and the naming of the National Conservation Area. Now, the river below Crystal Dam is all Gold Medal Water, which restricts the fishing to some degree, but overall makes for some quality fish.

The major trails into the Gunnison Gorge below the Black Canyon are Chukar, Bobcat, Duncan and Ute. They are all accessed from Peach Valley Road, east of Olathe and are all well marked. Presently, this is a fee area, so take along a few dollar bills.

Chukar Trail is considered to be a trail that lends to packing in boats. Good physical condition is a must though. This is not an easy thing to do, and once in, getting out is a problem unless you arrange a pick-up downstream. A call to the BLM office in Montrose will produce the necessary information regarding this activity.

I recall one trip to the river down the Chukar trail. No boats were involved. We fished all morning without any success. Keep in mind that this was before the advent of Gold Medal Waters. We had used about every fly we had and even tried some salmon eggs that day. Then I discovered one lonely grasshopper as I was trudging back toward the trail. I managed to catch the hopper in my landing net, impaled him on a number 6 hook with a couple of split shot sinkers and tossed him out into the river, letting him drift into a small back eddy. The result was the only catch of the day and was on the north side of five pounds. At the time, it was one of the biggest rainbows I had ever caught. Lesson learned: tie up some big old hopper patterns and keep them handy for trips into the Gunnison Gorge.

The next trail downstream from Chukar is Bobcat. This is a steep and difficult trail. It sort of switchbacks through a ravine and, at one point even has a rope to assist you down a drop of 20 or 30 feet. The amazing rock formations of the canyon walls on the far side of the canyon are worth the trip. Again, the fishing is good, although it has been years since I attempted this trail, I keep in touch with many who regularly use it. Do it while you are young and agile.

Duncan Trail is another rather difficult trail requiring about 1.5 miles of hiking from the top of the ridge to the river. All of these trails are good opportunities for overnight excursions.

Lastly, there is Ute Trail, which is much longer than the other trails, but much easier to negotiate. Once you get to the river there are over three miles of water to test your skills.

There are other trails but those are the most popular. Now, if you want a real trip, in more ways than one, make arrangements to visit Pleasure Park off of Highway 92 about 13 miles east of Delta. The park, which includes a private enterprise, is located at the confluence of the North Fork of the Gunnison with the

Gunnison. I do not endorse a lot of guides or outfitters, but a trip up the river with these people is a trip of a lifetime.

From Blue Mesa to Delta, the Gunnison River is the epitome of life in Western Colorado.

CHAPTER NINETEEN

McPhee and Navajo Reservoirs— Southwestern Gems

The San Juan River water backed up behind Navajo Dam is mostly in Colorado, but the dam is in New Mexico. The tail water of Navajo is legendary for the quality of fishing, but it is very popular and often crowded. Mid-week and non-holiday trips are good ideas.

I discovered crappie in the early 1970s, when I first visited Bonny Reservoir in extreme eastern Colorado. The pursuit of these members of the sunfish family is a little patchy in western Colorado, but opportunities do exist.

My first experiences with crappie left me with the impression that the best time to go after them is in the spring of the year when the water begins to warm and triggers the spawning action. The fact is there are some nice crappie to be had at about any time of the year, if you know where to go and how to fish for them. One of those places to go is McPhee Reservoir in Montezuma County.

McPhee is part of the Dolores Project. It dams the Dolores River and the water is used for irrigation in Montezuma County, Dolores County and the Ute Mountain Indian Reservation. While there are some shore-fishing access areas in the House Creek arm of the lake and near the edge of the town of Dolores, the lake is better fished from a boat. The dam was completed in 1985 and within a few years my dad and I tried it out. My dad grew up fishing for trout in small streams and lakes around Cripple Creek and Victor. Catching a crappie and getting it off the hook without driving a few spines on the dorsal fin into his hand was a new experience for Dad, but before long he became enthused about the simplicity of fishing a small jig fly under a bobber and catching some respectable sized fish. Besides, they taste good.

I have fished McPhee several times since that first trip with Dad, but that is the trip that stands out in my mind. For three or four years my employment required that I spend a lot of time in the Cortez and Durango areas. As is always the case, fishing took my mind off my work and gave me a chance to unwind. It was during that time that I discovered those few places around McPhee that offered a chance to catch fish without a boat. McPhee has several kinds of fish, including the hybrid strain of rainbow known as the McConaughy trout. Like most rainbows, I usually return those to the water for someone else to enjoy. My primary purpose for fishing McPhee is the crappie.

During one business trip I learned from a local outfitter that crappie can be caught during cold months too, but they tend to run deep. Because McPhee fills a canyon full of water and backs up into several river channels, there are certainly deep places for the fish. Find the shad and you find the crappie. During the warmer days of spring and early summer the fish move onto their spawning beds and are present in much more shallow water and around some of the many submerged willow thickets and other brushy cover. Do not leave your fly rod behind. Fishing these willow thickets from a float tube or a small inflatable pontoon is an ideal way to spend a few hours.

Since you have your fly rod anyway, you might want to try the tail water below McPhee. Prior to the building of McPhee, the Dolores River was in bad shape. It often dried up completely in some places, but the dam allowed for the control of the water and a fish habitat was literally reborn. The river is stocked with brown trout, rainbows and Snake River cutthroat. I could not believe how fast the fish took hold in that stretch of river. Within a couple of years after the water was flowing, the trout were worth catching. Early on, the fishing pressure was low, but certainly has increased over the years. I was told that there were a couple of bad years when the water was way too high, but I missed out on those years and have had mostly positive experiences on my trips.

There is another quality place to go in the southwestern portion of the state. Actually, while the water backs up behind Navajo Dam mostly into Colorado, the dam itself is in New Mexico. Various retail outlets on the Colorado side, near the border offer New Mexico fishing licenses. My tactic is to buy their five-day license so I can fish in both states.

Ask about anyone who owns a boat in western Colorado and they will tell you that they have been to Lake Powell at least once, and many of them will tell you that it is an annual occurrence. Those same people will often say that they have never been to Navajo Reservoir. I think the trip to Navajo is a much better bargain. While not as massive as Powell, and while it lacks some of the grandeur, Navajo is a great place to go. The dam blocks the San Juan River, which is a major tributary of the Colorado River. There are places where the water is nearly 400 feet deep and the scenery is great, as are the people. Some of the friendliest people I met were in the small town/marina of Arboles on the Colorado side of the border.

For the boater, the lake has it all. When full is covers about 15,000 surface acres. There are a number of tributaries, which offer some respectable smallmouth and largemouth bass, and of course, my favorite crappie. As with McPhee, the spring and early summer is a great time for the crappie, but they are caught in significant numbers throughout the year in the deeper areas of the lake.

My passion, however, is the fishing below the dam in the San Juan River. To say the fishing pressure is high on this stretch of water is an understatement. I have been there when it marvels me to just sit and watch all the fly lines being whistled through the air. How all those doing the casting manage to do it without tangling up their lines is beyond me. That being the case, with a little forethought about what day you want to go, it can still be fun. Avoid holidays and weekends whenever possible. October is a good month, but I often have to deal with a deer season about then too. Some of those decisions I have to make are excruciating. The fish are wary and the small flies seem to work best for me. Patterns of the caddis and stonefly are good choices and the small bead headed varieties of caddis or prince are not to be ignored.

The San Juan River above Navajo also has some good fishing, but there is a lot of private property and the fish seem to be somewhat smaller. There are some nice camping and RV parks available, and as a side attraction, the casinos at Ignacio and Farmington are not too far away to provide a nice side-trip.

CHAPTER TWENTY

San Miguel River— Summer and Winter

The San Miguel River, which flows through the town of Telluride and on down the canyon to its confluence with the Dolores River, has become a very popular destination for the trendy fly fishers of today. Don't discount this river for some great winter fishing. Access is better now than it has been for years and the rewards are always gratifying.

I would not be reluctant to claim that somewhere back in history one of my ancestors invented the picnic. As far back as I can remember my family, especially on my mother's side, has engaged in picnics. When we didn't have some special place to go, we simply went outside, spread a blanket on the lawn and had a picnic. When more than three or four family members get together even today the gathering usually involves some sort of outdoor meal and a fire.

Back in the 1950s, when uranium mining was booming in the west end of Montrose County, my mom's brother Bert and his family lived in Naturita. To say that Naturita had drinking water would be to claim something that was entirely untrue at the time. There is no way a person could drink what came out of the typical tap in a home in Naturita. Consequently, and because my parents lived in Ouray where the water was clean and pure, we often hauled cream cans full of water over to my aunt and uncle so they could have drinking water.

Uncle Bert loved to fish and he was good at it. He and his brother Erle were very instrumental in teaching me the basics of fly fishing and that of fly tying. It seems that Bert caught fish when nobody else did. He simply had a knack of finding fish and knowing what to do to get them into his creel.

Because we had to make a water delivery and because the San Miguel River just happened to be along the way, it was not unusual for our combined families to meet at some spot along the river, have a picnic and do some fishing. We kids loved the time we spent with our cousins and I particularly enjoyed trying to uncover the secrets of Bert's fishing. I learned a few of those secrets and they are going to remain secrets to some extent, but my biggest lesson was that, in order to fish a river, you must get in the river and wade. Of course, most of us kids were between three and eight years old at the time, and we certainly were not allowed to wade the river. Instead, we were relegated to sitting on a rock and drifting a worm through some pool over and over again until we finally caught a fish. Oh, we caught fish, but not nearly as many or any as big as those caught by Bert. I watched intently as he carefully waded out into the water and deftly placed a fly just right above a rock or downed tree and let the fly drift into the path of a feeding trout. I watched as his bamboo rod bent and he examined each fish to see if it were a keeper or not. It was not long before I was experimenting with doing a little wading on my own. By the time I was a young teenager, I thought nothing of getting into waist high water to reach a special spot. I began to look at running water in a whole new way. I pictured fish slowly moving their tails back and forth to maintain a spot where food could float by them, giving them nourishment without too much expenditure of energy. I had learned just a few of Bert's secrets.

I suppose those secrets are the reason that the San Miguel River remained a favorite of mine for many years, but as Telluride grew and fly fishing became somewhat of a trendy thing to do, the fishing pressure on the San Miguel became a problem during some times of the year. The regulations also changed and I fished the river less and less as the years went by. Occasionally, when my job required a trip through the area, I would stop at one of those wide spots, don my waders and fish for an hour or two. Because the river follows closely along the highway from Placerville to the Norwood Bridge, and because there are a number of public access points, the opportunity for a break in the daily routine is certainly there.

During those times when I fished the San Miguel as a kid, Colorado had a fishing season that started in the spring and ended in the late fall. Winter fishing was not a common thing and could only be practiced in a few locations around the state. For that reason, as much as any, I had little idea that any river could be fished in the winter. There were a few of us that threatened to try it but we didn't. Even after winter fishing became legal, I mostly concentrated on ice fishing, but I found an absolute treasure trove in both the Uncompahgre and the San Miguel Rivers, especially after the dam went up at Ridgway, greatly improving the Uncompahgre and a few of the pull-offs along Highway 145 were upgraded, making winter access to the San Miguel just a little easier. I even started taking some fishing equipment with me when I went hunting.

The new neoprene waders are a great advantage over the tennis shoes and blue jeans of my summer gear, and a must if you plan on venturing out into the cold water and getting to those sweet spots. I also use a wading stick that is attached with a long cord to my fishing vest, just in case it decides to take a little trip downstream. The last thing you want to do is fall into the river on a winter day.

As for the winter fishing, it is pretty much the same as any cold Colorado river during the winter. It does seem to me, however, that dry flies work a little better in the San Miguel than in a lot of other rivers and streams during the winter months. I like to use the Dun Mayfly patterns and the Blue Winged Olives, and of course those little midges are always good things to have around. The fish run in the 12-18-inch range, so keep those sizes in mind as you stalk through the water. Move carefully and slow, both for safety and to avoid spooking the fish. If you notice that someone else has splashed upstream ahead of you, forget that spot for a while.

The San Miguel runs about ninety miles from the base of the mountains in Telluride to where it dumps into the Dolores River a dozen miles or so east of the Colorado/Utah border. A lot of the river is accessible to the public, but there is a significant amount of private property too, including some mining claims. And, not to put a damper on things, but the only live rattlesnake I ever encountered in Montrose County was near the San Miguel River about a mile upstream from the Nucla power plant. I have heard stories of lots of other rattler encounters along the river and it is wise to be diligent. Some people tell me there are some nice catfish near the confluence with the Dolores, but I have never been there and done that. Maybe that is a trip that needs taken.

CHAPTER TWENTY-ONE

Ponds—Don't Ignore the Small Stuff

When the Montrose Airport expanded in the 1980s, a new gravel pit was established nearby. The result was a pond that was later developed into a park by the city. Small ponds around the state are ideal places to relax for a few minutes or hours and are generally kid friendly, making them a great place to get the youngsters interested in fishing and outdoor sports.

I recall a day when I was sitting in a motel room in Northglenn wondering what I was going to do for five hours while I waited for my next meeting. I went to the bar, ordered a beer and visited briefly with a friendly bartender. During the conversation I mentioned that I would rather be fishing. She told me about a nearby pond where her boyfriend had been catching some fairly nice bass.

It turned out that the pond she was referring to is a reclaimed gravel pit that was being developed into a rather nice park. The state stocked the little lake with various kinds of fish, including the bass. I did not even have a fishing rod with me, but there was a discount store not too far away. In less than an hour I had a cheap spinning rod and a very limited selection of bass lures. I went fishing, caught four or five nice bass and was late to my meeting—a perfect afternoon.

Almost every small community, and many of the larger ones, in Colorado have some sort of a pond or small lake nearby. Some are developed into family oriented fishing holes while others are part of a state park or wildlife area. They are perfect places to take youngsters fishing and they can offer some great recreation for us older kids too. Many of these places are handicap friendly and some others are limited in use to just young people.

Beaver Lake (just one of many with that name) near the town of Marble is a popular place for easy access fishing, but not far away are a couple of small ponds that are often overlooked by those who fish the lake. McKee Pond is a small pond situated near the Marble airstrip. It is home to some pretty impressive brook trout. I drove by this pond several times because I knew it was on private property. I then noticed a sign informing visitors that, while the pond is on private property, it is stocked by the state and is open to public fishing. That is all I needed to know. While a number of other people drove by that day, there was only one other person fishing the pond. My subsequent visits have had similar results.

While I do not really consider it a pond, Confluence Lake in Delta is a great place to take a couple of kids and teach them the basics of fishing. It is also a great place to take a lawn chair and a can full of worms. The surrounding park has volleyball courts, a swimming hole and numerous picnic areas, but sometimes it is possible to sit among a crowd and be all alone. As a rule the fish are going to be stockers, but I use barbless hooks and return them to the water for another time.

Near Paonia is a small pond located within the Volunteer Park complex. This is one of those places where fishing is limited to the young. In this case, those under 14 are encouraged to take advantage of some fun sunfish populations. It is a wonderful place for casting instruction and is not heavily used. Once a year the U.S. Fish and Wildlife hatchery near Hotchkiss sponsors a fishing derby for the children of the area. They stock the pond with a truckload of trout for the derby, so there is always the possibility that some young upcoming angler can latch on to one of those big retired brooders that are sometimes put into the pond.

There are those days when the river below Ridgway Dam is crowded with fly-rod totting enthusiasts practicing their best catch-and-release strategies. Just to the north of the parking lot are two ponds where bobbers and hooks are welcome. Again, take a kid along and it becomes just that much more fun.

When my three sons were growing up in Montrose, both my wife and I were working and the boys, as boys do, became bored. We encouraged them to get on their bicycles and go to Chipeta Lakes for a couple hours of fishing. Since that time the area has been taken over by the Colorado Parks and Wildlife and the lakes (plural) have become one lake. CPW routinely stocks the lake with rainbow trout, and both large and small mouth bass. This is another place where a fishing derby is held each year, leaving a few of those stockers for us folks needing a respite from our daily routines. When I first acquired a small inflatable pontoon boat, it was Chipeta Lake where I first tested it. It was relaxing to just float around in the middle of the lake and catch a fish or two. Just hang a sign on the door and go fishing.

Many of these ponds that I refer to are the result of gravel mining activity. After the gravel is removed the holes often fill naturally with water, making the transition to a fishing hole fairly easy. One word of caution: if the shoreline has not been altered to accommodate you otherwise, the banks can be steep and falling in will put you in deep water almost immediately. Be careful.

One of those gravel pits-turned fishing hole is a small pond in the Taviwatch Park on the north edge of Montrose. When the Montrose airport was expanded several years ago, the gravel came from what became the park. Adjacent to the pond is the manufacturing facility for Scott Fly Rods and it is not unusual to see someone from that company testing a new rod—or maybe he is just hanging that sign on the door. At any rate, the edges of the pond have been modified some so the slope is much flatter, making it another fine place for kids. It is also a popular place to train bird dogs and for dog exercising in general. Fish in the pond include some impressive sized small mouth bass.

The final word is that these small bodies of water can mean relaxation for a few minutes or a few hours. They are part of my mental health as much as they are part of my recreation.

CHAPTER TWENTY-TWO

Lost Lake—Or Should it be "Found Lake?"

The U.S. Forest Service brochures brag that Lost Lake and Lost Lake Slough are homes to an abundance of wildflowers and they are not exaggerating. The area is also one of the most beautiful in Colorado during the fall when the aspens and scrub oak display their hidden splendor.

I have to admit that I made more than one trip to the area just off of Kebler Pass in Gunnison County thinking that I was at Lost Lake when I was actually at Lost Lake Slough.

A lot of the lakes and ponds on Grand Mesa and the surrounding forests bear the name "slough," which really refers to a marshy area rather than a full-fledged lake, but I had nothing to do with the naming and I suspect that those names had much more to do with claiming the water than identifying a lake or pond. Many of the sloughs are nothing more than shallow marshes, but Lost

Lake Slough ranks a little higher in my book and is a very good place to fish.

My purpose here is to bring attention to the fact that we do not have to travel great distances to experience some quality scenery, good fishing and occasional tranquility. Lost Lake fits that criteria, but it really is not lost, at least not any more. The high usage prompted the U.S. Forest Service to completely revamp the Lost Lake campground, which by the way is closer to Lost Lake Slough than to Lost Lake, but Lost Lake is not far away.

The campground gets some heavy usage and is often full over a weekend, especially if it is a holiday weekend. It is a very popular place for local families to gather and it is kid-friendly. Motorized boats are not allowed on the lakes in the area, but float tubes and small hand-propelled craft can be a lot of fun. The good news is that, even if the campground is full, there are often open campsites along the two miles of Forest Service Road #706 leading up to the campground.

The forest service brags in its brochures that Lost Lake has an abundance of wildflowers and they are not exaggerating. Depending on the time of the year, just about every native flower known to the Colorado high country blooms in the area. It is a great place to take the kids and a wildflower identification book. But all that has nothing to do with fishing.

Lost Lake Slough is stocked regularly with catchable sized rainbows and it has a good population of natural brook trout. The brookies can reach some impressive sizes, but seem to be a little hard to come by as the summer wears on. A short hike to the south of the slough is Lost Lake. Here the crowd gets a little smaller and the surrounding scenery gets even better. A fly rod and some standard dry flies might lead to several hours of great fishing and those home-bred brook trout are even better. Every one I caught was solid and healthy feeling. If the fly rod is not your thing, a small ultra-light spinning rod and a bubble and fly rig is a good choice for these small lakes.

Not far from lost lake to the southeast is the smaller Dollar Lake, which is accessed off of the main trail and is a fairly easy slope down to the lake. There are even fewer people at Dollar Lake, although I have witnessed a small tent or two tucked back into the trees. Again, the catch of the day will be those great tasting brook trout. The main trail is the Three Lakes Trail (#843) and is well marked. It is also well used by hikers. It always amazes me how few of these stick-walkers carry a fishing rod. I am not complaining. I am just commenting.

The main access to the area is on Gunnison County Road 12, either from the Paonia side or the Crested Butte side. This route over Kebler Pass is popular, especially during the height of the fall season when the colors are as good as any place in Colorado. My suggestion is to try to get to this area during mid-week and to avoid holidays. The Independence Day weekend is way too popular for my blood. Memorial Day is often too early anyway, but Labor Day is a no-no unless you are going with a group and planning to have a good time with a lot of people. Gunnison County does a fairly good job in keeping the road maintained but it gets rough in places and it is not uncommon to hit patches of washboard. After turning off of County Road 12 onto Forest Service Road 706 it is time to really slow down if you are towing a camp trailer, but it really is not a bad road into the campground. As I mentioned above, the forest service put a lot of effort into the campground in 2012 and 2013, so the road is somewhat better now than it used to be.

CHAPTER TWENTY-THREE

The Grandby Reservoirs— Taking the Rough Road

The Grandby Reservoirs, seen here from the rim on the Mesa Top Trail, are some of the best fishing lakes on Grand Mesa. While the road to the lakes is rough, the trip is more often than not worth a little bone jarring.

Photo is courtesy of gjhikes.com.

I have been on some of the hairiest, narrowest, highest and steepest four-wheel drive roads in Colorado but I do not think any of them compare in just plain roughness to the road going into the Granby Reservoirs on the south side of Grand Mesa.

The Grandbies, as they are known, are a group of small lakes located south of the well-known Island Lake. The road begins just beyond the Island Lake campground and is only a road in the technical sense of the word. It is mostly a lot of rock jutting out of hard volcanic formations. If I were a geologist, I would likely spend a lot of time analyzing this, but I fish and hunt, so I will spare everyone the explanations given me by experts relating to basalt outcroppings, toreva slumps and pre-historic landslides. Suffice it to say that all those things do not make for a smooth road, but the water and the way it is trapped at various places on Grand Mesa makes for some great fishing.

I first ventured into Grandby Reservoirs when I was in high school using a two-wheel-drive pickup. I later made the trip a couple of times with an old friend in his 1946 Willys Jeep.

The Jeep was a little better than the pickup, but my last few trips in on the back of an ATV were much less bone jarring.

This is a trip best scheduled for sometime after the middle of June when Mother Nature has had some time to take care of the last of the snow. Early in the summer you will have less of a mosquito problem, but sometimes I think those little buggers stay awake all winter just to torment me and Grand Mesa has a reputation of having some major mosquito populations. I never go there without plenty of DEET.

There are several lakes in the Grandby group. Some of them are only accessible by foot (or horseback if you are so inclined), but others are literally beside the road. As you approach the area on the forest service road (115), the first lake you will encounter is number 11. The road runs pretty much the entire length of the lake on the west side and there are ample opportunities to stop and walk to the edge of the lake. I always stop a few times going in and sometimes on the way back out, depending on the success.

The next lake close to the road is number six. This is one of my favorites. West of number six is the larger number 12. In my experience number 12 is the first lake of the group to get full of moss and weed. I rarely fish there. If you follow the road beyond number six you will eventually come to the Big Battlement Lake. While not technically part of the Grandbies, this is a great fishing lake. Both number 11 and Big Battlement are good places for small inflatable boats and float tubes.

Take a good map and a GPS receiver with you on these trips and, if you are so inclined, walk into some of the other lakes. The scenery is great and the fishing can be fabulous.

I prefer to use light spinning equipment when I go into these lakes. My favorite method is using a bubble and fly rig. My uncle told me the Danish fishermen first used this method. He may have claimed that because of his Danish heritage, but it works.

Because I have mentioned the bubble and fly rig so many times, let me explain how I do it: First I use a light or even an ultra-light rod with a good monofilament or equivalent line. I select a water bubble that is about the size of my thumb. I prefer the type that allows the line to be fed through the center so it slides. Just below the bubble I attach a small swivel. This keeps the line from twisting and acts as a stop for the bubble. I then attach about six to nine feet of light leader. Remember that, the longer the leader, the more difficult landing a fish becomes. I like to have the leader short enough that holding the rod above my head brings the end of the line out of the water.

Sometimes I simply tie my favorite fly to the end of the line and start fishing. When I am fishing anywhere on Grand Mesa when the mosquitoes are out, I add very well treated dry mosquito fly to the line about halfway between the swivel and the end. I often use some type of a beaded head or a wooly bugger fly on the end of the line to start with and change as conditions dictate, but I usually leave the mosquito in place, sometimes even re-applying dry fly treatment now and then as the day goes on.

All of the lakes in the Grandby complex are renowned for the presence of native cutthroat trout. These beautiful fish are fun to catch, good to eat and challenging to find. Like so many higher altitude lakes, the Grandbies are finicky, but when they are giving up their fish, they can represent one of the best places in Colorado to fish—rough road or not.

CHAPTER TWENTY-FOUR

The Lake Fork of The Gunnison— and How to Stop Chewing Tobacco

By putting the camera on a nearby rock and setting the timer, I was able to record a small part of a hike up the North Fork of the Gunnison. The photo reminds me of that week in August of 1985 when I quit chewing tobacco.

As the snow melts from the side of Handies Peak, one of Colorado's famous "fourteeners," the water flows into Sloan Lake and then flows out, creating the Lake Fork of The Gunnison River.

I remember hiking into Sloan Lake only one time. I do not even remember who accompanied me, but I do remember that the water was so clear that one could stand on a gray rock cliff above the lake and see the rocks on the bottom. Now and then a fish would slowly rise to the surface and barely break water. I do not remember catching any of those fish, but I have several fond memories of times way below Sloan Lake along the Lake Fork.

During my teen years, one of my favorite activities was taking a trip over either Engineer or Cinnamon Pass. When Vernon and Irene Wrye bought the theater in Ouray, I was working there as a projectionist. The Wryes were from Cleveland and were fascinated with the beauty of the San Juan Mountains. One of their first orders of business was to purchase a new Jeep and I became a self-appointed guide, making sure that Jeep had the opportunity to try every rugged four-wheel drive road in the area. The trip to Lake City over Engineer or Cinnamon certainly qualified as rugged and the scenery from the top is astonishing.

On one of our trips we took along Bill Catlin, a sound technician from Denver, and his 80-year-old uncle who was in the U.S. visiting from England. Old Uncle had never experienced much of anything outside an English big city. He held on to the "chicken bar" from the time we left Main Street in Ouray until we arrived at the small restaurant in Lake City where he pronounced that he "bloody well" needed something much stronger than root beer if we planned on returning to Ouray over the same road. We took the long highway route back to Ouray. Blue Mesa Dam was just over one year old at the time and the real fishing of the reservoir had not yet begun.

After the Lake Fork tumbles down from its lofty beginning, it flows through Lake San Cristobal, just south of Lake City. San Cristobal was formed hundreds of years ago when a huge rockslide created a natural dam. Not everyone you talk to will know that it is the second largest natural lake in Colorado, only Grand Lake in the headwaters of the Colorado River is larger.

I fished San Cristobal many times from the shore. In the 1980s I took a boat one time, but I was alone and the boat motor acted up, so a fishing trip became a repair trip. I later ventured out on San Cristobal in a canoe. That, also, was a frustrating trip. I relegated myself to fishing from the bank on the few occasions that I returned thereafter.

As the Lake Fork leaves the Lake City area, it offers several opportunities for the fishing enthusiast, but the fact is that most fishermen that fish the river today do so by boating up from Blue Mesa Reservoir. Several times I ventured up the Lake Fork in a boat to a point where the river was no longer navigable. On one such trip we encountered a literal log jam where the trees and debris were floating in the water in a huge circle. My dad and I first decided to turn around, then changed our minds and got out the spinning rods. We hit a honey hole just below the log jam and spent an hour or two catching some very impressive brown trout, along with a rainbow or two. We trolled our way back to the main lake and did not catch near as many fish during the trip back as we did in that time among the driftwood.

I may well have the Lake Fork to thank for whatever good health I have.

I cannot even remember how old I was the first time I put a little pinch of Copenhagen in my lip and began a habit that I kept for years. For many of those years I did not have any desire to quit chewing. In fact, I actually thought at one point that spitting a little tobacco juice on a worm improved the chances of a fish wanting that worm. I guess fish have some bad habits too.

In August of 1985 I finally decided that I was going to give up chewing; not because I really wanted to, but mostly because it was becoming a fad that I did not want to be associated with. The "Marlboro Man" had been kicked off of television in the early 1970s and it seemed that every wanabe stud, along with a significant number of girls, were "taking a pinch instead of a puff." And the idiots were spitting everywhere, including into cups while they stood in line to load their plates with food. Enough was enough, but quitting was not easy.

After trying to quit chewing at least a dozen times, I decided to do the thing that so many times had rescued my mental health from the bottomless pits of despair—I went fishing.

I loaded a backpack with a few essentials, including a zip-lock bag of cornmeal and another of Crisco. I left a brand new can of Copenhagen on my dresser and had my wife take me to the Lake Fork Bridge at Blue Mesa. I spent the better part of three days walking up the Lake Fork, fishing and then, after the sun went down, reading *North and South*, written by John Jakes. I stared into a fire for hours and nearly ripped off a shirt pocket trying to find a can of chew.

I ate or released the fish I caught and returned to the highway at the designated time to catch my ride back home. My expedition caused more than one eyebrow to rise among my peers at the Montrose County Sheriff's Office, but I finally kicked the habit that weekend and the Lake Fork of the Gunnison River will always hold a special place in my heart.

CHAPTER TWENTY-FIVE

Cochetopa Creek—Connecting With My Ancestors

The early spring presents a challenge for fishing Cochetopa Creek, but any time of the year is a good time to try your luck on this small tributary. While much of the lower creek passes through private property, there is some access allowed after permission is granted by the landowner.

If you have been reading thus far, you no doubt have figured out that I will use about any excuse I can to go fishing. Sometimes my reasons are justified and sometimes those who love me so much seriously question them.

One justifiable trip several years ago took me south on Colorado Highway 114 from its intersection with U.S. Highway 50 east of Gunnison to the town of Saguache. My primary purpose was to locate the Alaska-Yukon Mine, which is located just above Camp Kettle Gulch about 2.5 miles south of the Gunnison/

Saguache county line. The side benefit was the discovery on my part of another fun fishing destination.

My great-grandfather, Peter Smith Saunders was the superintendent of the Alaska-Yukon Mine in 1915 when he was struck ill and went to the hospital in Gunnison. Two months after his admission, he was still in the hospital and died there on November 15, 1915. Just prior to his death my grandmother and her two sons (my dad's half brothers) drove from Cripple Creek to Gunnison via horse and buggy to visit him. He was buried in Gunnison because transportation of his body back to the Cripple Creek and Victor district was too complicated.

I sometimes think I sound like a broken record, talking about the water in Colorado and where it comes from. The fact is that there is no place within this fine state where water flows in. All the water rushes down off these beautiful mountains in a hastened goal to reach either the Arkansas or Colorado drainages and exit the state. Luckily for some of us, there were people who slowed the water down and figured out ways to store it. The original reason in most cases was to provide for agricultural longevity in the state, but fish like water and we all get a side benefit.

San Luis Peak just barely reaches that all-important 14,000 feet of elevation and it is on that lofty summit that Cochetopa Creek is born. As the creek wanders down through Cochetopa Canyon, it is largely on public lands, but also flows through a significant amount of private property. The creek is stocked by the state, and as such, some of the private land is accessible after permission is granted from the landowner. On one of my trips I happened to see one of the landowners nearby and asked if I could fish the small section of the creek that flowed through his property. He was not only amiable, giving me permission, but was interested in my family heritage in the area and topped off an interesting and informative conversation by pointing out a couple of great little fishing holes.

There are several places along Highway 114 where you can pull off and easily get to the creek. There are also some formal and not-so-formal camping areas dispersed along the route and part of the creek flows through the Cochetopa State Wildlife

Area. Within the boundaries of the wildlife area parking is limited to designated parking spots and access from the road is limited to shank's mare or those real horses that some are inclined to cajole into carrying them by giving ample quantities of alfalfa and oats.

Cochetopa Creek is one of those extremely clear flows of water. It may get a little murky at times, but I have never witnessed it in that state. As expected, it will run a little heavy in the spring, but it always seems to be clear. So, if you are a splashy wading fool, you will likely go without hooking up many fish. This creek requires some stealth while also requiring that you spend some time in the water. The banks are lined with some serious brush, mostly willows. Wading slow and easy and watching for the subtle trout hideaways is the secret to success.

This is not a place where you can show off your ability to make hundred foot casts. The back cast from a nine foot fly rod will get you little more than a few willow leaves or set your hook into a branch that is way too high to reach. Those little roll casts from a shorter rod are much more effective. I like to use the various attractor flies on this creek, but don't hesitate to make a dropper fly with some kind of weighted nymph or bead head. If the timing is right and you get there during the willow fly hatch, this little creek can turn out some nice browns. I surprised myself once with a 14 incher, but most of the time they run about eight to ten inches long.

As a side, if you venture into the Cochetopa SWA, you will also have access to some good fishing on both Los Piños and Archuleta Creeks. Again there is some private property involved, so act like a good guest so the rest of us do not suffer.

When you get tired of walking, take a few minutes or hours and visit the Dome Lakes SWA, accessed via a well-marked side road off of 114 about 22 miles from Highway 50. These lakes have good shoreline and do not seem to be heavily used, although I have never been there during a long holiday weekend, so that may be a different story.

Regardless, this is a good place to pull out the lawn chair and a sandwich, sit back and relax.

CHAPTER TWENTY-SIX

Finding Your Fridstool

Mount Hayden, as seen from the rooftop just outside the bedroom that I occupied while growing up in Ouray, Colorado. I spent many hours sitting on that rooftop reading a book or just daydreaming. It is probably the first example of my "fridstool," although it was many years later before I put a name to it.

The good thing about being familiar with the area in which I live is that I can jump into my pickup, hook on to a travel trailer and/or an ATV trailer and head for the hills. Most of the time my little excursions are not well planned. They are more likely to be spur-of-the-moment things and likely not far from home.

I have often written about the therapeutic value of fishing, hunting or just spending time in the outdoors; time that some may think has no real purpose. When things get a little hectic, either with my job or with things in general, I can bring everything back into perspective with a few hours in some remote spot. Actually, it really does not even need to be remote. It just needs to feel remote.

I became a fan of Diana Gabaldon. She compiled a series of books that are an interesting mixture of history and fantasy with a little time-travel thrown in. In one of her works, *The Scottish Prisoner*, I learned a new word. I had never heard it before, but given her penchant for insertion of historical facts into her work, it is likely an old word that just has not been used for a few centuries. The word is "fridstool." One of the characters in the book defines the strange word as being a "seat of refuge" or a "sanctuary" where one can go and be alone with one's thoughts.

I have several fridstools. Most of them are in or near the San Juan Mountains, but there are some that are much more readily accessible and quite often used. The important thing about a fridstool is that it does not have to be a secret place. It just has to be a place where one has every chance of being alone. Now, by being alone, I have to say that I exempt my dog from that requirement. He seems to know when I am sitting on a fridstool and he seems to be more than willing to comply with the requirement that I just want to be away from people.

If you go fridstool hunting, look for a place that instills calmness. Look for a place where you can share the beauty of what is around you. Look for a place where your imagination can roam with the breeze and return with amazing ideas. Look for a place where you feel alone, even if you are not. Then allow the place time to soak in and communicate with your inner being. Some would say this is a form of meditation, but meditating brings on memories of the 1960s when I watched too many people meditate themselves into a life of being worthless. So, I prefer to use my newly found word and describe my little excursions as just sitting on my fridstool.

When I venture out to one of my fridstool locations. I may, if the season is appropriate, take along a shotgun, just in case a turkey decides to present itself at an opportune time. I almost always take along a fishing rod, just in case I come across a good-looking stream or lake, either going or coming, and I often take my dog. We may frolic a little in some high altitude snow or I may throw a few Mepps spinners in a small stream. We might visit one of the easily accessible high lakes for a little fishing either before or after a visit to the fridstool. I often build a small fire and roast a couple of hot dogs. Very often my fridstool is right there at the site of the fire.

My mind is always refreshed as the result of a fridstool visit. Just a few hours seems to rejuvenate me and calm me down. I return home ready to tackle the real problems of life with a little different outlook. I still have no idea what Gabaldon's fridstool really looks like, but I know how it feels to sit on one.

CHAPTER TWENTY-SEVEN

The Thunder Mountain Connection

Alexander Lake is one of the many easily accessible lakes on Grand Mesa. There are nice campgrounds nearby and some delightful commercial entities. The only caution is to remember the insect repellent. The mosquitoes on Grand Mesa are legendary.

Legend has it that Grand Mesa was referred to by the Ute Indians as Thunder Mountain. I have no way of knowing if that is really true, but it makes for great folklore and it suits me just fine to accept it as at least plausible. In my notes I also have information that the Utes called Grand Mesa "Thigunawat," which translates to something like, "Home of departed spirits." I like the legend that goes along with the Thigunawat tale, whereby the many lakes on Grand Mesa were formed when some old Ute displaced a bunch of vicious thunderbirds, throwing them out of their nests into the waiting jaws of a giant serpent. The thunderbirds prevailed and tore the serpent up, dropping parts of its body on top of Grand Mesa, creating many indentations that ultimately filled with water.

I attended a seminar some time back in which the geologists and forest service rangers said little about the thunderbirds, giving us all an explanation that involved erosion and volcanic activities being the reasons for all the lakes. Frankly, I cannot go up the side of Grand Mesa without looking in the sky for the spirits of those thunderbirds.

Undisputable is the fact that the word "mesa" in the Spanish language means "table." So, early referrals to Grand Mesa as being called "Table Mountain" are probably accurate for the time.

I am here to tell you that Grand Mesa is not flat on top. It has beautiful miniature valleys, canyons and uplifts and is covered with all types of vegetation. The wildlife ranges from the smallest birds and gophers to moose, the giants of the deer family.

At any rate, Grand Mesa did not get much attention until the early settlers of the Grand Valley and surrounding areas began showing up in about 1881 and began vibrant agricultural endeavors. Growing things requires water. Water flows downhill. All those indentions on Grand Mesa were full of water. An irrigation system was born.

Many of the lakes were modified to hold more water. Ditches and pipes followed and Grand Mesa became a very important source of life-giving moisture to the crops below. It also began providing recreation to its surrounding residents, especially those who supported the sport of angling. It was more than 100 years after those first settlers began their move that I began appreciating the beauty and splendor of Grand Mesa.

Prior to graduating from high school in Ouray, I made only a few trips over Grand Mesa, mostly to go to Collbran, and to fish at Vega Reservoir or to venture into the Granby Reservoirs. With those exceptions, I did not spend much time on Grand Mesa.

That began changing after I moved to Montrose in 1980 and made one more trip into the Granbies with a stop at Island Lake and a short hike from there to Little Gem Reservoir. I began seeing the potential of Grand Mesa and made a number of trips over the next few years.

In 2002, when I took over at the *Mountain Valley News* in Cedaredge, Grand Mesa became even more important to me. I could then take an afternoon off and do some serious fishing. While the opportunities to do a lot of hiking to access remote lakes and ponds certainly exists, some good fishing is available just a few yards from your vehicle. You can take an afternoon, a day or several days to just drive around and stop a few minutes here and there to cast a line. Taking a small boat or floatation device makes it even better.

Get yourself a good map and play a little "hooky" with me. Starting at the intersection of Colorado Highway 65 and Colorado Highway 92, just east of Delta, travel through the small towns of Cory, Eckert and Cedaredge and head up the "scenic byway" that is Grand Mesa. About 9 miles from Cedaredge is the first body of water that is very obvious to the casual traveler. Ward Creek Reservoir is literally right beside the road. This is a good place for that quick sandwich while wetting a line or two. The catch is going to mostly be those fish stocked for our enjoyment, but they are fun to catch.

The next stop on my little hooky-playing trip is Cobbett Lake, again right beside the road. Cobbett is roughly six miles above Ward Creek Reservoir, just before the highway makes a big bend and heads off to the west. Cobbett is one of the smaller lakes and tends to moss up pretty bad later in the year, but it is a nice place to fish. Because of its proximity to the visitor's center, Cobbett is always popular with the young traveling families.

Just around that sharp corner you can travel along the north and west side of Island Lake. The turnoff to the lake and campground is well marked. If you have your boat with you, this easily becomes a place to spend the rest of the day. It is popular and mid-summer will give you a chance to meet people from all over the country, but my little trip leaves Highway 65 at Cobbett, which is where the visitor's center is located. So turn at the visitor's center and head east on Forest Service Road 121. There are some private enclaves along this route, so pay attention to your map and the signs. There are a few access points to Deep Ward Lake along the road just a short distance from the visitor's center, but I have not fished there much. Just beyond Deep Ward is Alexander Lake. Again, some private ground, but there is adequate access to provide a few minutes of fishing here and there. There are a lot of cabins and business enterprises around Alexander and the nearby Hotel Twin Lake, so don't get sidetracked.

Continuing on via FS121, stops might include Baron and Eggleston Lakes. There are several places along the shore of Eggleston where you can literally drive to the edge of the water. Next is Young's Creek Reservoir number three and then on to where BB50 Lane intersects with FS121. A short side-trip here ends at Trickle Park Reservoir, one of my favorite places along this route.

Leaving Trickle Park and back to FS121, watch for the intersection of FS125 and turn right. A short distance from the intersection you will again see Trickle Park Reservoir and have opportunity to fish on its northeast shoreline.

Trickle Park is usually my last stop on this little trip. FS125 heads back south, eventually becoming Surface Creek Road, then a turn onto Ute Trail Road brings us back to Highway 65 and back to Cedaredge.

A couple of words of caution: Take this trip quickly the first time and decide on the places you like most. There are a number of campgrounds in the area, making it possible to turn this into an excursion of several days. Get a good map and take advantage of some side trips if you spend a few days. Lastly, the mosquitoes on Grand Mesa are legends in their own rite. Take along plenty of good insect repellant.

Grand Mesa is the epitome of fishing close to the bank. Depending on what information you read, there are between 300 and 500 lakes on top of the mesa. In addition, there are miles and miles of small streams and beaver ponds. Some of the lakes are fished heavily, some are remote and can be as tranquil as heaven itself.

Chapter Twenty-Eight

Island Acres—Getting Over Spring Fever

Diane and I were married in 1969. She grew up fishing with her father and at least pretends to enjoy fishing with me now and then. Her preference is bait fishing. The most complicated piece of equipment she has is a small closed-face spinning reel. Actually, I fully understand how just sitting and waiting for a nibble can be called fun.

About the middle of March of each year I start getting a little antsy. Oh sure, I have had some deer and elk hunting and a couple of ice fishing trips, maybe a rabbit hunt or two over the winter, but there is something about March that starts my blood moving differently.

As I sit in my home office with one window looking out over my deck and the skyline broken by a large elm tree, I begin to notice little things. The small hulls from the elm buds begin to show up on the deck and in the dog's water. A robin or two land in the apricot tree and sit close to each other. The male doves begin to bow to their chosen partners and my lovely wife begins to hint about what needs done outside before summer hits us hard. It will not be long until the hints become much stronger.

My travel trailer sits and waits for me to inspect it. I start hoping that it survived the winter and that I was successful in getting all the water out of the lines and that the battery accepted the trickle charge from the small solar panel. No sooner do I get inside the trailer than it begins to almost pulse with the desire to hit the road. A long trip is not needed, just a short one or two day excursion strictly for testing purposes. A couple of days not too far from home to find out if everything works is always a good idea, and I may as well throw in a little fishing while I am at it.

Wife Diane likes to fish. What she does not like are lots of bugs and needing to go potty in the woods. We evolved through our camping years with a lot of fun and memories and things improved as we went along.

First, we did the tent thing. The kids were young and it was an adventure of sorts each time we pitched a tent. We went from the heavy canvas tent wrapped around an aluminum frame with everyone inside to the "easily" pitched dome tents that always seemed to have a broken pole or two.

Our first camper was a converted school bus. It was also a lot of fun, at least until I blew a hole in one of the pistons while returning to Bethune from a trip to the Cheyenne Mountain Zoo. I rebuilt the engine myself and enjoyed the bus for another year or two. We used it to move to Montrose in 1980.

From the bus we advanced to a pop-up camp trailer, then our first camp trailer, which we bought after it was abandoned at a local RV camp. We found a substantial amount of "green leafy substance" while cleaning it out. That was not a good thing. At the time, I was an investigator in charge of narcotics investigations at the Montrose County Sheriff's Office, but I digress. From that old camper, we eventually advanced to a brand new 23-foot with a slide-out living area. The most important thing after the tents was that we have a usable toilet; Diane insisted on that.

Camping in March is not always an easy thing, but it is not impossible. One merely has to take advantage of what is available. That is where Island Acres comes in. Island Acres is part of the James A. Robb—Colorado River State Park and is located off of Exit 47 of Interstate 70, just east of Palisade. I can leave my house and be at Island Acres in about an hour. There is just enough difference in climate to make a trip to Island Acres possible before other places are accessible. The campground is rarely crowded in March or early April and it makes a good place to check things out.

There are several ponds. The biggest is regularly stocked with rainbows and is a good place for the kids. Diane likes to fish but casting a fly or using a spinner are not things she is prone to do. She relates well to a lawn chair, a bobber, some bait and some sunshine. She also seems to enjoy catching bullhead catfish, which are self-sustaining in the pond designated as Bullhead Flats.

Bullheads like water that is not so clear. They even do well in somewhat brackish water. They are bottom feeders and, like their bigger catfish cousins, they depend on scent to find food, so if it smells dead and rotten, they will find it and try to eat it. Just about anything that a person eats will be eaten by a bullhead, but the more it stinks the better they like it. Chicken livers are good, as are the various catfish dough baits. An old friend of mine mixed up some stuff made of cornmeal, rabbit blood, garlic and chicken livers. He added just a pinch of brewers yeast and left the concoction sit in an open jar in a warm place for a couple of days before putting the lid on. Caution: If you mix this stuff up, take along some surgical gloves to handle it with. My hands smelled of the stuff for days after I used it, but we caught fish.

You do not need a lot of expensive tackle to fish for bullheads. A rod, a line, a hook and a sinker or two will get your bait to the bottom. After you catch one of these ugly things, be sure to avoid the spikes on the dorsal and side fins. They will sting you, and don't put your fingers into their mouths. I like to use a small pair of locking pliers to grab them by the lip for hook removal and later for skinning, which is usually better than fileting for this size of fish. Fix them up just as you would any catfish. Battered, grilled or part of a jambalaya, they make a good meal.